THE RENEWAL
OF COMMON PRAYER

OF RELATED INTEREST

Published by SPCK

Edited by Michael Perham

TOWARDS LITURGY 2000   Preparing for the Revision of the Alternative Service Book   1989   £7.99

LITURGY FOR A NEW CENTURY   Further Essays in Preparation for the Revision of the Alternative Service Book   1991   £6.50

MODEL AND INSPIRATION   The Prayer Book Tradition Today   1993   £3.50

Published by Church House Publishing

THE WORSHIP OF THE CHURCH   as it approaches the Third Millennium   A Report of the Liturgical Commission   GS Misc 364   1991   £1.25

GS Misc 412

THE RENEWAL OF COMMON PRAYER

Uniformity and Diversity in Church of England Worship

Essays by members of the Liturgical Commission of the Church of England

Edited by Michael Perham

This volume has only the authority of the Commission by which it was prepared

GS Misc 412

First published in Great Britain 1993
Society for Promoting Christian Knowledge
Holy Trinity Church
Marylebone Road
London NW1 4DU

and

Church House Publishing
Church House
Great Smith Street
London SW1P 3NZ

British Library Cataloguing-in-Publication Data

A catalogue record for this book is available
from the British Library

ISBN 0 281 04712 X (SPCK)

0 7151 3754 9 (CHP)

Printed in England by Orphans Press Ltd., Hereford Road, Leominster, Herefordshire.

Contents

The Members of
the Liturgical Commission
April 1993

The Right Reverend Colin James, Bishop of Winchester (*Chairman*)

The Venerable Mark Dalby, Archdeacon of Rochdale

Mrs Molly Dow

The Reverend Canon Roger Greenacre

The Right Reverend Patrick Harris, Bishop of Southwell

Baroness James of Holland Park

The Venerable Trevor Lloyd, Archdeacon of Barnstaple

The Reverend Canon Michael Perham

The Reverend Stephen Oliver

The Reverend Canon Jane Sinclair

The Reverend Dr Bryan Spinks

The Very Reverend David Stancliffe, Provost of Portsmouth

The Reverend Dr Kenneth Stevenson

The Reverend Canon John Sweet

The Reverend Michael Vasey

Dr Susan White

Consultants
The Reverend Canon Dr Donald Gray

Brother Tristam SSF

Secretary
Mr David Hebblethwaite

One of the contributors to this book, The Very Reverend John Gladwin, Provost of Sheffield, is not a member of the Liturgical Commission.

Foreword

Common Prayer is a fashionable issue in the Church of England. And it is not difficult to see why. People are concerned with the preservation of ancient and familiar texts that we have prayed in common. Such texts have nourished people's spirituality, and have formed a kind of treasury from which they could draw in times of need. Moreover the actual concept of common prayer is dear to many, the idea that there is a body of material that Anglicans use in their worship which constitutes a source of unity and identity.

Without wishing to minimise the importance of these concerns, we need to recognise that in reality there never was as much common prayer in the past as we sometimes now imagine. There has always been diversity and variety. And this book tells that story with care. And it also needs to be stressed that the recent liturgical history of the Church of England has not been the determined march away from common prayer that is sometimes portrayed. On the contrary in a number of ways, particularly with the establishment of the Parish Eucharist as normative, the worship in ordinary Church of England parishes may well have more in common than in previous generations. Admittedly there may be more variety in the texts that are used, yet in the style and ethos there has been a convergence. And at certain key points in the year Anglicans in England are probably using more in the way of common text than for a long time, partly through the provision of books like *Lent, Holy Week, Easter* and *The Promise of His Glory.*

Nevertheless, without being naive or simplistic about the past, or seeking to repudiate the desirable freeing up of worship in recent years, there is an issue to be addressed. The Church needs to reflect on what are the proper limits of liturgical diversity. And it needs to ponder on the nature of its common prayer. It is significant that it is being urged to do this, not only by those who are most concerned with the conservation and use of older forms, but also by those involved in the creation of new liturgy, not least by members of the Liturgical Commission itself. One dares to express the hope that by reflecting on these issues the Church may come to an agreed mind on the form and extent of its common prayer, combining a reverence for tradition and an openness to new material that can take its place within this core. If this hope can be realised then the Church could be well served by forms of worship that will emerge in the year 2000. Well served not only for praying its liturgy, but for its doctrine and its unity also.

+ COLIN WINTON

PART 1

1
Introduction

Common prayer is part of the Church of England's heritage. By it Anglicans have meant a sufficient degree of uniformity in liturgy that people, moving around the country, may find in any church a family likeness in worship, involving words and music, structure and ethos. For a long time common prayer was synonymous with the Book of Common Prayer. But the issues of common prayer and the 1662 Prayer Book are separate, though connected. The Roman Catholic Church, for instance, has a large measure of common prayer right across the world, through its breviary and missal, but these are not historic texts hallowed by use through the centuries. At least as far as translation is concerned, they are thoroughly contemporary. But there is common prayer.

The liturgical life of the Church of England in the last generation has seemed to be marked by an undervaluing of common prayer. The desire to make the liturgy fit its local culture and the spirit of an age that has put much emphasis on freedom and variety has resulted in too little attention to common prayer, and to what might be lost with it, should it be further eroded.

But there has been in very recent years a growing recognition of the need to maintain, and, if need be, restore common prayer for the spiritual health both of the Church and of individual Christians. In this book of essays, members of the Liturgical Commission set out to show what the concept of common prayer has meant through Anglican history, to demonstrate why its maintenance is crucial today, and to discuss what form it should take. For though many would welcome a return to a greater consciousness of

3

common prayer, few would advocate the degree of uniformity which many imagined to be a natural part of the Church of England a generation or so ago.

But why is common prayer so important for the Church's well-being? There are at least three distinct reasons.

Firstly, it is important for pastoral reasons, and some of these are discussed in Chapter 5. In our very mobile society, people need to find the familiar in terms of structure and text as they travel from place to place, or as they tune in to broadcast worship on radio or television. People need also to be set free in the liturgy from the need to be constantly studying a service sheet or book, and that too implies familiar structures and memorised texts. People need also, at times of stress or illness, to be able to draw on a reservoir of material that lives deep within their soul, and that can only be built up through a growing familiarity with the material. The spontaneous and the variable have much to commend them, but they cannot be the staple diet of the soul.

Secondly, common prayer is important for the Church's *koinonia* or fellowship, not so much within a particular congregation, where much else may hold it together, but nationally and internationally. Traditionally Anglicans particularly have looked to their liturgy as something that binds them together, creates family likeness, and holds them in unity and fellowship. Indeed it was in the past the Book of Common Prayer, seen as a distillation of one strand of the Western liturgical tradition, that as much as anything cemented together Anglicans the world over, living in a variety of cultures but holding to one communion. In time each Anglican province developed its own Prayer Book, but the new books were nearly always derived from the English Prayer Book of 1662, and liturgical revision was carried on with an eye to what was happening elsewhere in the Anglican Communion.

If that has been true internationally, and still is to a lesser extent, something of the same truth applies within England itself. Liturgy is still one of the most powerful forces for unity and fellowship in the Church. Although there is more textual variety than in the past, and that might seem to have undermined common prayer, there is still a remarkable family likeness to Anglican worship in England, and in terms of the style and ethos of eucharistic worship possibly more sense of common identity than for a long while.

But the third reason for defending common prayer is, in the end, the most crucial. It is that common prayer protects the doctrinal integrity of the Church. Anglicans, asked what they believe, point not so much to a confession of faith as to a set of services. Alongside the Thirty-nine Articles of Religion as a reference point there are two other documents where Anglican doctrine is to be found, and both are liturgical – the Book of Common Prayer and the Ordering of Bishops, Priests and Deacons (appended to the Prayer Book, but technically not part of it). If there is no common prayer, there is danger of a loss of common doctrine. If each may devise their own service form and write their own prayers, then each may make their own doctrine. If we look to our liturgy to show what we believe, liturgy shapes and reflects doctrine. That places a heavy responsibility on the liturgist, but it also means that liturgy needs to be properly authorised, so that sound doctrine is both assimilated and protected. Of course this danger can be overstated. It is possible to have common doctrine without common prayer, as evidenced by the Puritans and Presbyterians from the seventeenth century onwards. But Anglicanism would be a very different sort of church if its doctrine ceased to be found primarily in its liturgy.

For all these reasons – relating to pastoral needs, communion and doctrine – common prayer remains central to the Church's life. For the Church of England this means holding on to traditional forms of common prayer and also seeking new ways of expressing it today. This book is not chiefly concerned with the issue of holding on to the traditional forms. It is not a plea for a more central place for the Book of Common Prayer of 1662 – not that the Liturgical

Commission is unsympathetic to that plea. We are here concerned with a broader issue, which is not dependent on a particular book however hallowed by use, but in its recent exchange with the Prayer Book Society (in *Model and Inspiration*, SPCK 1993) the Commission has said

> The Commission shares the view that the Book of Common Prayer and the Authorised Version of the Bible should remain in the mainstream of Anglican worship and, to the extent that this has not been so in the last generation, the Commission believes that Anglicans need to take seriously and to recover their heritage.

But, in the more general way, the concern has been to define and to build a strong 'evolving common core' in Anglican worship that will still leave room for legitimate variety, experiment and local decision. If the basic need for common prayer is accepted, and if the concept of the evolving core wins approval, the debate then focuses on the size and content of that core. The members of the Commission believe that this whole area is a vital one for the Church and want, by the publication of *The Renewal of Common Prayer*, to encourage real debate about these issues, not just among those who will make decisions in synods about the future direction of liturgical revision, but also among those who order worship in parishes across the land, and who by the decisions they take protect or endanger the Church's common prayer and identity.

The Commission set about writing *The Renewal of Common Prayer* in this way. It appointed a group of four – Archdeacon Trevor Lloyd, Canon Michael Perham, Canon John Sweet and the Reverend Michael Vasey – to see the project through. This group commissioned contributions from others and later went through every essay and suggested amendments to the author. They also took the drafts to the full Commission. Each essay bears the name of its author, but has also been carefully scrutinised by the group of four, and discussed more generally by the full Commission. We have not asked every member of the Commission to assent to every word in the book, but the whole Commission happily 'owns' the book and encourages its study in the church.

Chapter 4, 'Image, Memory and Text', bears the names of three commission members, and all three of them have written parts of that chapter. They were tackling a particularly sensitive issue, and, starting from rather divergent viewpoints, they spent several meetings in a successful search for agreement among themselves. Their signatures together at the end of the chapter are indicative of the common mind that has emerged in the Commission.

One of the chapters is not by a member of the Commission. The group of four was sufficiently struck by a contribution in the General Synod by the Provost of Sheffield, the Very Reverend John Gladwin, on the subject of common prayer and its relation to its social and political context, that it asked him to turn his thoughts into a contribution to this book, and this he has done in Chapter 5. We are grateful to him for joining us in this enterprise.

The book is in two parts. In Part One, five descriptive essays come at the common prayer issue from different angles – in terms of history, literature, culture and ecumenism – while a sixth essay (Chapter 7), still descriptive in style, provides a necessary corrective to the picture that emerges. The picture is completed in Chapter 8 by John Sweet's theological reflection. These essays are intended to be primarily descriptive, and they build up a full picture in which there are few contradictions, but the authors have been given the freedom to indicate something, not much more than a hint, of future strategy. There is a striking convergence, but there is also an intentional reticence in working through the implications until we reach Part Two of the book.

Part Two of *The Renewal of Common Prayer* opens with a long chapter that is very much the heart of the book. Here

Michael Vasey, to whom the Commission is much indebted for his enthusiasm for this project, draws together the material from the earlier chapters, and sets out the Commission's conclusions about the options the Church now has before it. This chapter comes as near to a policy statement as a Commission wanting to initiate a debate can come, and the material within it has been the subject of more frequent discussion and scrutiny by the whole Commission than any other part of the book. The two final chapters fill out the message of Chapter 9 in terms both of the leaders of worship and also of the people who come to worship. There is a proper balance struck between the need for stability and for change, and a concern for good training, education and formation.

This is inevitably a very English and very Church of England sort of book. It is saved from being wholly insular by Donald Gray's contribution on ecumenical common prayer in Chapter 6, and this introduction has already noted the world-wide Anglican dimension. We live at a time when we are being pressed to celebrate our distinctiveness, as John Gladwin argues, yet with a determination to be inclusive rather than exclusive. There is a proper and legitimate Englishness to our liturgy even as we rejoice to be part of the catholic Church. There is also a distinctive Anglican dimension to English Christianity, but we share our translations of scripture, our hymns and much else of our liturgical heritage with the other Christian Churches in our land, and nothing that we have written here, in trying to discern what is right for our own Church, should be mistaken for lack of concern for our wider relationships with Christians of other traditions or cultures. If we do celebrate our distinctiveness, it is as a contribution to something greater, and with a yearning for a sense of common prayer that embraces the whole Church of Christ.

MICHAEL PERHAM

2

Anglican Identity and Church of England Worship Today: An Historical Reflection

FLEXIBILITY AND ENRICHMENT

What goes on in parish churches up and down the land excites easy comment, whether it is a national occasion, an ordinary baptism, or when something more unusual is taking place. Anglicanism has long known variety. The 1662 Prayer Book, after all, is an embodiment of an organic development, which introduced, at the eleventh hour, two gems of Anglican devotion, the General Thanksgiving and the Prayer for All Sorts and Conditions of Men. Beneath the surface, too, there lurks a parallel development, which is about adaptation: abbreviation and curtailment on the one hand, and supplementary material on the other. Some of these resulted from theological climates, such as the Enlightenment, followed by the Evangelical Revival, in the eighteenth century; and the Tractarian Movement in the nineteenth. Evangelicals introduced hymns – an entirely new feature – and Tractarians added new (and old) prayers and ceremonial. How the Prayer Book was actually used in the parishes has been a varied picture.

In our own century, two tendencies have become apparent. The first is about the desire for flexibility, so that the received text can be adapted to suit local circumstances. In the 1920s, this was particularly manifested in the revision of Morning Prayer, whereas today it is more obvious in the eucharist.

9

The second tendency is the desire for enrichment. In the 1920s this concerned alternative canticles and additional collects and prayers. Sometimes enrichment had another motivation – to correct the inherited Prayer Book theology, as in the case of some of the additions to the eucharist produced by Anglo-Catholics. Now it focuses also on alternative eucharistic prayers and forms of intercession.

But it is the same process. In recent years an additional twofold pressure has been brought to bear. On the one hand, the 1974 Worship and Doctrine Measure liberated the Church of England from some of its historical shackles, bringing it slightly nearer the other provinces of the Anglican Communion. Such a Measure was bound to produce a desire to affirm creativity! And the drift towards 'you-language' in the late 1960s all over the Communion was bound to result in an explosion of new material.

The historian, looking at this scene, has to take a long view. Many years ago W. H. Frere, in commenting upon the way liturgies grow and change, drew attention to the 'oscillation of movement'[1] between fixed and free, between those ages characterised by new ideas and material and those which are known for their relative firmness. It would seem to be inevitable that our own age of creativity should be followed by one which searches for some kind of stability.

SHAPE VERSUS CONTENT

One of the most brilliant books on worship published this century was Dom Gregory Dix's *The Shape of the Liturgy* (1945).[2] Among the many things he taught was that the liturgy is essentially a series of actions, which are interpreted by words. It was a needful insight from which the Church of England could benefit: worry less about 'getting the words right' and concentrate more on the inner meaning of the eucharist. I thought of Dix one St Benedict's Day (11 July) in the home of two of my parishioners when I celebrated the eucharist. They are long-standing, devoted churchgoers, theologically astute. They delighted at the occasion, not just because of Benedict but because I was going to anoint one of them. For the liturgy, I used a simplified version of one of the cards in *Patterns for Worship*.[3] There it all was: the liturgy presented shape-wise, like the agenda for a meeting.

But it was not just 'shape' that nourished the occasion, it was 'content' too. It mattered that Ted and Shirley (and the celebrant too!) knew a basic core of the service by heart, without confusion, without the distraction of having suddenly to work hard, in a context where there was enough fatigue anyway. So the knowledge of the Collect for Purity, the ASB Confession, the Prayer of Humble Access, as well as the Sanctus and Benedictus, the Lord's Prayer, and that all-too-brief Post-Communion Prayer, was of vital importance, because for Anglicans content is indeed important. But our literary culture produces a basic expectation that, whatever kind of person one is dealing with, we need to know where we are in the service in church.

THE EFFECTS OF VARIETY

Anglicanism has long known variety, and its many motivations. Over and above all the churchmanship issues there comes the simple fact that England today is a pluralistic society, entering what the jargon calls the 'post-modern' age. In this kind of world, it would be prudent to ask, what is liturgical variety doing to people, to the Church at large?

Variety tends to destabilise if it is too frequent. People need a sense of security when they worship, with a common core, which is made up of shape and content. Once that is established, they may be ready to experience other elements. But if they get too much variety at once, the material is likely to be discarded as debris, either because it is indigestible, or because the material itself does not 'meet their needs'. (How often is the most tucked-away intercession in *Patterns* actually used? How many lovers of the Prayer Book are familiar with the Commination service?) This is not to suggest that what is not used should no longer be printed. Another age may come along with excitement and rediscover something lost or forgotten – history is full of that dynamic.

But when variety determines the content of a liturgy, it functions more effectively if the shape is mandatory. Anglican worship in this country would be immeasurably improved if we had an ASB more like the 1979 Book of Common Prayer of the Episcopal Church of the USA,[4] where the *shapes* of services are much more stable. People are more likely to be able to cope with alternative prayers, eucharistic prayers, canticles, intercessions, if they know exactly where they are likely to come.

There is an issue of liturgical formation here: once there is a rhythm, there is a greater chance of people expecting the liturgy to make sense. Worship leaders could serve the Church well by giving some basic teaching about why certain items come into services, and what they might mean. It is quite possible to preach teaching sermons that do not impose very specific meanings on features of liturgy but leave congregations grasped by the artistic and liturgical quality of prayers at their best. If one takes into account Frere's 'oscillation of movement', a strong sense of shape and a basic core of content, and even adds good teaching, one is still left with the basic question of the need for variety. The Byzantine rite has long known two forms of the eucharist, and has easily coped with them because their shapes are identical and the main congregational responses the same. The Liturgy of Basil in Lent and at festivals happily replaces Chrysostom, which is the normal diet.[5] History teaches again and again that variety in presidential (and other ministerial) parts is easier to cope with than too much variety in the congregational parts.

HYMNODY

Anglicans have a curious history over hymnody which is quite at odds with Methodists, to say nothing of Lutherans. Charles Gore had grave difficulties with *The English Hymnal* when he was Bishop of Oxford, because it contained what was (for him) material at variance with Anglican tradition.[6] But the world has changed since the early years of this century. Hymns are written and they are sung, whatever authority says, and whatever the words might embody, and they provide Anglicans with a legal and semi-liturgical way for new material to be appropriated, adapted, or discarded. Perhaps there needs to be much more monitoring of words and music of hymns and choruses.

One of the reasons for the importance of this issue, apart from the sheer quantity of material being produced by musicians and lyric-writers at the moment, is the often quite distinct roles which hymns and chants, however broadly interpreted, play in the overall act of worship. In former years, the hymn was primarily a song of praise, even if its mood and content were affective and devotional. Nowadays, there are some items, for example, a Taizé chant, which are repeated many times, rather like the thrice-sung 'Kyrie eleison' of the Byzantine *ektene,* with the result that it can create an intense atmosphere of prayer and adoration which liturgical styles of recent years have found difficulty in engendering on their own. Such chants are often, moreover, the 'background' of worship, unlike many of the songs and choruses of the 'Renewal' tradition, whose words and music are often in the 'foreground' of worship.

These shifts in liturgical music need to be noted for what they are doing to worship in general, and also what gaps they are filling in people's devotional lives. There is nothing necessarily un-Anglican in all this, especially as Anglican liturgical texts have themselves been eclectic in their sources from the very beginning, in the Book of Common Prayer of 1549.[7]

PRESENTATION

Anglicans have long had a reputation for doing the liturgy well. But what are the criteria for describing ceremonial, simple or elaborate?

One way was suggested many years ago by Bishop Frere, who expounded three types. The first is functional, where something is done because it has to be done, like the president walking into church. The second type is symbolic, where the gospel-book is carried down among the congregation, symbolising the proclamation of the Good News to all people. A third is allegorical, where the whole eucharist is an allegory of the life of Christ, with the Gloria in Excelsis re-enacting the Nativity and the Consecration as the Crucifixion.[8] On this basis, Anglican ceremonial is usually functional, frequently symbolic, but never allegorical.

Another way is to distinguish between different approaches to what is directed in the service books themselves. The Prayer Book tradition is not prescriptive here, in the way of the 1570 Roman Missal, which is quite specific about every movement, gesture and posture of the priest. Nor is it suggestive, in the way of the 1970 Roman Missal, which copes with variety by suggestion, prescribing only where it is deemed essential to do so. Anglicans, by contrast, have their own approach of a minimalistic kind, which recognises the reality of ceremonial pluralism – of variety of presentation – and enables the liturgy to take root and flower unselfconsciously in very different contexts. Our way of doing the liturgy does not exist in the abstract; it needs to find a climate and memory of its own in order to embody an appropriate style.[9]

There remains, however, the important issue of architecture. Many church buildings are being re-ordered, but how many of them demonstrate in one glance the traditional Anglican arrangement of font, reading desk, pulpit and altar – and all visible? Baptismal tanks that are opened up for occasional use often remind me of the eighteenth-century holy tables, tucked away in distant sanctuaries, dwarfed by three-decker pulpits! Visitors to our churches, occasional or frequent, need to *see* lectern, pulpit, font and altar, as obvious and essential pieces of furniture for the use of the People of God.

Much more work is required on liturgical presentation, at three levels, presidential and ministerial, typographical, and contextual (architectural!). It is a well-known fact that there are areas of European Catholicism that took all the more easily to the Vatican II reforms because they had been well prepared for them by priests who knew what they were talking about, eucharists celebrated from the 1570 rite in a way that anticipated what was to come, and in buildings tastefully adapted. Buildings, texts, and ministers together are themselves a 'concelebration' of worship at its widest and deepest.

CONCLUSION

It is perhaps appropriate that one who was nurtured on the Scottish Prayer Book of 1929, with its eucharistic oblation and epiclesis,[10] should draw attention to the fact that any discussion about identity that is a mature reflection on a religious story needs to articulate the purpose of being a Christian community at all. To celebrate the sacrifice of Christ and to call upon the Holy Spirit to enable us to be the instruments of God lies at the heart of Christian theology. Put in ecclesiological terms, this means seeing the Church as a self-offering, Spirit-filled, but always for the purpose of redemption.

The Church, on this view, is not meant to be self-serving. Discussion about identity in any part of it must have a functional rather than an ontological character to it. Churches seeking communion with each other across historic divisions obviously are at an advantage if they have a common core of doctrine and liturgy, made up of shared shapes and contents. Once that discussion concentrates on one particular Church, it needs to embody both what that Church has in common with the Church Universal and what that Church has which is distinctive and enriching for the others.

Anglicanism has a wealth of both. It has much in common with historic Christianity, particularly the Churches of the Catholic and Reformation traditions. But it has evolved its own ethos. Such an 'identity' is a continually evolving one. In our own century this is bound to involve the tension of handling an explosion in the art of prayer-writing and also of doing the liturgy well – both text and context. That requires discernment, a spiritual gift that is the result of the ear of fine-tuning. Liturgical memories are handed down almost unconsciously from one generation to another. That means safeguards are not everything, and liturgy develops its own climate organically.

But we do need a basic core of material that we can say is both Catholic (in the widest sense of the term) and distinctively Anglican (our own domestic ethos). My own suggestion is that, in the severely practical terms of an 'irreducible minimum', this should consist of the bare bones of the statutory services, together with certain elements that are common to all, or can be used in all (the Lord's Prayer on the one hand, the General Thanksgiving on the other). But these can only be the instruments: self-offering and invocation of the Spirit are the primary themes of all worship.

KENNETH STEVENSON

NOTES

[1] R. C. D. Jasper (ed.), *Walter Howard Frere: His Correspondence on Liturgical Revision and Construction,* Alcuin Club Collections 39 (SPCK: London 1954) p. 195 (taken from a memorandum on liturgical revision written by Frere in 1920).

[2] Gregory Dix, *The Shape of the Liturgy* (London, Dacre/A. & C. Black, 1945). See also Kenneth Stevenson, *Gregory Dix – 25 Years On,* Grove Liturgical Study 10 (Grove Books: Bramcote, Notts 1977), pp. 23-35.

[3] *Patterns for Worship: A Report by the Liturgical Commission of the General Synod of the Church of England* (GS 898: Church House Publishing: London 1989) pp. 42ff. (This particular text is a simplified version of the Rite A eucharist.)

[4] See *The Book of Common Prayer* (Church Hymnal Corporation/Seabury: New York 1979). See also Marion Hatchett, *Commentary on the American Prayer Book* (Seabury: New York 1980), *passim*. The central question of shape is particularly obvious in relation to the 'Rite 3' (for informal occasions) liturgies for eucharist, marriage, funeral.

[5] See Hugh Wybrew, *The Orthodox Liturgy: The Development of the Eucharistic Liturgy in the Byzantine Rite* (SPCK: London 1989).

[6] See G. L. Prestige, *The Life of Charles Gore* (Heinemann: London 1935), pp. 300ff.

[7] See any of the pages of the main text of F. E. Brightman, *The English Rite* I and II (Rivingtons: London 1915), where the left-hand pages include, in the first column, the sources, the second, the text of 1549, and where the right-hand pages include the texts of 1552 and 1662. The variants are clearly indicated. The whole book is an object lesson in the evolution of classic Anglican liturgy, from varied sources, through main editions and editorial alterations, to definitive version in 1662.

[8] See W. H. Frere, *The Principles of Religious Ceremonial,* Oxford Library of Practical Theology (Longmans: London 1906), where chapters VII–X differentiate between these three types, with historical and theological illustrations.

[9] See David Stancliffe, 'Is there an "Anglican" liturgical style?', in Kenneth Stevenson and Bryan Spinks (eds.), *The Identity of Anglican Worship* (Mowbray: London 1991), p. 133 (whole essay, pp. 124-34).

[10] The literature on the development of the Scottish Episcopal eucharistic prayer is prodigious: see the classic treatment in John Dowden, *The Annotated Scottish Communion Office* (Grant: Edinburgh 1884); see also the relevant portions of Kenneth Stevenson, *Eucharist and Offering* (with foreword by Mark Santer) (Pueblo: New York 1986).

3

The Reformation Prayer Book Ideal

CRANMER'S SINGLE USE

The full title of the book published in 1549 was 'The book of the common prayer and administration of the Sacraments, and other rites and ceremonies of the Church: after the use of the Church of England'. Here 'the common prayer' is apparently distinguished from 'the administration of the Sacraments, and other rites and ceremonies of the Church', and it could be interpreted as referring only to Mattins and Evensong, along with the Litany and Suffrages. Cranmer's Preface (reprinted in 1662 with the title 'Concerning the Service of the Church') might support this interpretation. It drew significantly from the preface to Quinones' 1535 revision of the Roman Breviary. It speaks of the way in which 'the common prayers in the Church, commonly called divine service' had been corrupted, but its specific illustrations of this corruption all relate primarily to the daily offices.

On the other hand, the 1549 Act of Uniformity speaks of 'Mattins, Evensong, celebration of the Lord's Supper, commonly called the Mass, and administration of each of the sacraments, and all their common and open prayer',[1] and the book itself has a rubric about 'the divine service, appended to the rite of 'The Supper of the Lord'. A few years later, the 1562 homily 'Of Common Prayer and Sacraments', traditionally ascribed to Jewel, clearly equates 'common' prayer with 'public' prayer and explains, 'To pray commonly is for a multitude to ask one and the self thing with one voice and one consent of mind'.[2]

18

There were therefore in 1549 and immediately thereafter two different understandings of 'common prayer', the restrictive and the broader, and each had good historical precedent.[3] But in popular usage the long title of 1549 and its successors was quickly abbreviated, and this had two consequences: the broader usage became almost universal, so that 'common prayer' was not limited to one part of the book, and the concept of 'common prayer' was identified with 'The book of the common prayer'.

In the last resort, of course, this identification cannot be sustained, and it is perfectly possible in our own day for a multitude 'to ask one and the self thing with one voice and one consent of mind' whilst using the 1980 Alternative Service Book or some other form. But to Cranmer the whole idea of alternative books was anathema, and he wrote in the 1549 Preface:

> Where heretofore, there hath been great diversity in saying and singing in churches within this realm: some following Salisbury use, some Hereford use, some the use of Bangor, some of York, and some of Lincoln: Now from henceforth, all the whole realm shall have but one use.

If we are to understand Cranmer's ideal, we must look not only at the nature of 'the common prayer' but also at 'the use of the Church of England'.

Cranmer's reference to the 'great diversity' which had prevailed heretofore was exaggerated. The various English medieval uses had their differences, but these were hardly great and in no sense fundamental. The 1549 Act of Uniformity makes clear that there were weightier matters behind the insistence of 'one use' for 'all the whole realm'. It refers to the divers medieval uses, but points out that 'besides the same now of late much more divers and sundry forms and fashions have been used', and if some were pleased therewith others were greatly offended. The King had 'divers times essayed to stay innovations or new rites ... yet the same has not had such good success as his highness required', and it was 'to the intent a uniform quiet and godly order should be had' that he had appointed the Archbishop of Canterbury and other learned men to 'draw and make one convenient and meet order, rite and fashion of common and open prayer and administration of the sacraments'. Parliament was mindful of 'the honour of God and great quietness, which by the grace of God shall ensue upon the one and uniform rite and order in such common prayer and rites and external ceremonies', and it prayed the king that all ministers should be bound to say 'all their common and open prayer, in such order and form as is mentioned in the said book, and none other or otherwise'.

'Great quietness' was linked in the act with 'the honour of God'. But it also had what today we would call political overtones. Since the ending of the War of the Roses and with the establishment of the Tudor dynasty, there had developed a growing consciousness of nationhood. The royal supremacy in matters of religion, which followed the break with Rome, was part and parcel of this and was an English manifestation of the principle *Cuius regio, eius religio*. The 1549 Act of Uniformity expressed a sensitive concern for those who had been 'greatly offended' by unauthorised innovation, but the new prayer book was itself an innovation: the real agenda was that of authority.

As the Preface introduced the 1549 Prayer Book, so the explanation 'Of Ceremonies, Why some be abolished and some retained' concluded it. Some ceremonies, it was argued, were unprofitable abuses which 'much blinded the people, and obscured the glory of God'. These had been rejected, but others, though devised by man, pertained to edification and had been retained.

And although the keeping or omitting of a ceremony (in itself considered) is but a small thing: Yet the wilful and contemptuous transgression, and breaking of a common order, and discipline, is no small offence before God. 'Let all things be done among you' (saith Saint Paul) 'in a seemly and due order'. The appointment of the which order, pertaineth not to private men.

Again, the real agenda was that of authority, and the wilful transgression of a common discipline by private men was far more serious than the keeping or omitting of a ceremony. Indeed, 'Of Ceremonies' went on to explain,

> In these all our doings we condemn no other nations, nor prescribe anything, but to our own people only. For we think it convenient that every country should use such ceremonies, as they shall think best to the setting forth of God's honour and glory.

It was not that certain ceremonies were invariably right or invariably wrong. Each nation had to judge for itself – but the judgement was always to be made by competent authority. Only in the spheres of physical gesture and private prayer was a measure of freedom allowed. Appended to 'Of Ceremonies' were 'Certain Notes', one of which stated that 'As touching kneeling, crossing, holding up of hands, knocking upon the breast, and other gestures: they may be used or left, as every man's devotion serveth, without blame.' There was also a rubric at the end of the rite for the Lord's Supper which ordered people to occupy themselves during divine service 'with devout prayer, or Godly silence and meditation'. In all else there was to be uniformity, determined and enforced by competent authority.

But Cranmer and the Church of England were not alone here and, where England led, the Papacy was soon to follow. As a result of the Council of Trent, commissions were set up to revise the Roman service books, and the 1568 Breviary and the 1570 Missal were imposed by Pius V on all churches whose current rites could not claim an uninterrupted usage of at least two hundred years. Between England and Rome, therefore, there was no controversy as to the desirability of uniformity. The only question at issue was whether it was the Crown or the Papacy which could impose such uniformity and determine the contents of what was imposed.

THE AGE OF ELIZABETH

In Elizabethan England, however, it was Puritans rather than Papists who posed the main challenges, and in 1572 the Puritans launched a major offensive with *An Admonition to the Parliament*. Here, they complained that

> In the old church ... ministers were not tied to any form of prayers invented by man, but as the spirit moved them, so they poured forth hearty supplications to the Lord. Now they are bound of necessity to a prescript order of service, and book of common prayer in which a great number of things contrary to God's word are contained.[4]

Much of the controversy centred on particular prescriptions like the observance of holidays, and those who argued for the prayer book pattern were forced to fight on two fronts: that Cranmer was right in his detailed judgements and that, in any case, it was not for private individuals to take the law into their own hands. But at a deeper level the controversy concerned the propriety of liturgical worship as such, and here Richard Hooker commented:

> Of all helps for due performance of this service the greatest is that very set and standing order itself, which framed with common advice, hath both for matter and form prescribed whatsoever is herein publicly done. No doubt from God it hath proceeded, and by us it must be acknowledged a work of his singular care and providence, that the Church hath ever-more held a prescript form of common prayer ... so that ... it may be easily perceived ... that the public prayers of the people of God in churches thoroughly settled did never use to be voluntary dictates proceeding from any man's extemporal wit.

It was from Satan that there had proceeded 'a strange conceit, that to serve God with any set form of common prayer is superstitious', for God himself had laid down the form in which his priests were to bless the people, and our Lord had left us a pattern prayer.[5]

This section of *Ecclesiastical Polity* was published in 1597, not quite fifty years after Cranmer's first Prayer Book. During the next fifty years the Prayer Book was to enter still more deeply into the English bloodstream. The Prayer Book party then began to develop a new apologia, based neither on authority nor antiquity but rather on specifically spiritual considerations, and this came to the fore after the Restoration. Thus in 1672 Thomas Comber wrote:

> We may better pray by the Spirit in the words of a Form, than we can do, when our Mind is employed in inventing new expressions. For having a Form (which custom hath made familiar) we have all things set down to our Hands which we or others want; and we are at leisure to improve the good Motions of the Spirit; having no more to do but to join our Souls and Affections to every Petition, and follow them up to Heaven... It argues more of the Spirit of God, when we can attend the old Prayers with Zeal and Love, than when we need Variety and novel Expressions, to screw us up into a Devotion too much like Artifice.[6]

Nine years later, in *A Sermon on the Excellency and Usefulness of the Common Prayer,* William Beveridge declared similarly:

> Whatsoever good things we hear only once, or now and then, though, perhaps, upon the hearing of them, they may swim for a while in our brains, yet they seldom sink down into our hearts, so as to move and sway the affections, as it is necessary they should do, in order to our being edified by them. Whereas, by a set form of public devotions rightly composed, we are continually put in mind of all things necessary for us to know or do; so that is always done by the same words and expressions, which, by their constant use, will imprint the things themselves so firmly in our minds, that it will be no easy matter to obliterate or raze them out ... Having the form continually in my mind, being thoroughly acquainted with it, fully approving of everything in it, and always knowing beforehand what will come next, I have nothing else to do, whilst the words are sounding in mine ears, but to move my heart and affections suitably to them, to raise up my desires of

those good things which are prayed for, to fix my mind wholly upon God, whilst I am praising of Him, and so to employ, quicken, and lift up my whole soul in performing my devotions to Him.[7]

In 1689 the Act of Toleration was passed, and the ideal of 'one use' for 'all the whole realm' was formally abandoned. But for the Church of England the 1662 Act of Uniformity remained in force for more than three hundred years – though it was softened by the Act of Uniformity Amendment Act of 1872, which allowed the midweek abbreviation of the Prayer Book forms and the use of additional forms on other occasions, and by the Prayer Book (Alternative and Other Services) Measure 1965, which allowed the Convocations to authorise alternative services for periods of seven years.

Today the Act of Uniformity has been repealed, and contemporary Anglican worship is governed by the Church of England (Worship and Doctrine) Measure 1974, which gives permanent power to the General Synod to authorise services alternative and additional to those in the Book of Common Prayer. 'One use' even for the Church of England has now been abandoned. The Alternative Service Book, which is only an alternative to the Book of Common Prayer and which coexists with such Series One and Series Two services as are still authorised, makes as much use of 'may' as of 'shall', and just as the invention of printing made possible Cranmer's ideal of 'one use', so the development of printing technology has made possible a vast variety of texts. If *Patterns for Worship* is authorised, this variety (of forms as well as texts) will be increased yet further.

THE LESSONS OF HISTORY

But before we turn our backs wholly on the past, there are lessons to be learned and questions to be raised.

First, there is the question of authority. Contemporary authority lacks the bloody sanctions which it enjoyed in Tudor and Stuart times. Today it needs to be sweetly reasonable, and it can enjoin only that which commands widespread assent. Yet very few Anglicans favour total liturgical anarchy, and the propriety of individual ministers pursuing their own whims regardless of the Church as a whole is as questionable as ever.

Secondly, there is the concept of the nation. 'The whole realm' still has meaning, although it would need a sociologist to unravel that meaning. For the most part we speak of 'society' rather than 'nationhood' today, and it is increasingly apparent that ours is a pluralistic society – pluralistic not only in that it embraces people of all faiths and none but also in that it embraces a great diversity of culture even among those who stand in the mainstream of Christianity. Thus there are significant differences, in Church as well as community, between the city centre, the inner city and the suburban estate.

But the pluralistic society is also a mobile one and, as in 1549, what pleases some causes great offence to others. 'Great quietness' can no longer be linked, as then, with a rigid uniformity, but it is questionable if it can be achieved if there is unlimited diversity. Hence the urgent contemporary debate about the nature of common prayer. It may be that *Patterns for Worship* is right, and that the essence of common prayer consists of a common structure or a common core. But it may also be that Cranmer and Hooker, Comber and Beveridge, were right, and that common prayer involves common texts as well.

Whatever our answer to these questions, we can hardly be content with the status quo. We are confused when we recite the Lord's Prayer (1662, Rite B or Rite A?), and we are equally confused when we reply to the greeting, 'The Lord be with you'. Here at least, and arguably at many other points, the absence of a form 'which custom hath made familiar' is a positive hindrance to that unselfconscious prayer which has been a blessed hallmark of traditional Anglican devotion.

MARK DALBY

The Renewal of Common Prayer

NOTES

[1] Text in H. Gee and W. J. Hardy, *Documents Illustrative of English Church History* (London 1921), pp. 358-66.

[2] *Certain Sermons or Homilies* (London 1864), pp. 375-8.

[3] Cf. for a magisterial discussion F. E. Brightman, 'Common Prayer', *Journal of Theological Studies*, X.497-528.

[4] W. H. Frere and C. E. Douglas (eds.), *Puritan Manifestos* (London 1954), p. 11.

[5] *Ecclesiastical Polity*, V.xxv.4; (Oxford 1850), i.515.

[6] *A Companion to the Temple*, 1701, vol. 1 preface, cited from J. R. Wright, *Prayer Book Spirituality* (New York 1989), p. 32.

[7] Cited from P. E. More and F. L. Cross, *Anglicanism* (London 1935), pp. 626f.

4

Image, Memory and Text

LAYERS OF DEVELOPMENT

Our response to language is intensely subjective. Words and phrases which to one person convey a sense of majesty and awe will to another be archaic, elitist and unhelpfully obscure – if indeed they ring any bells at all – while the more simple sentences and cadences which adequately serve the needs of some worshippers will, to others, be banal and uninspiring, and devoid of that sense of mystery which, to them, is an essential in the worship of God. These differences of perception, rooted in personality and nostalgia, as well as in tradition, education and culture, exist apart from more esoteric and philosophical considerations of the nature of language and whether it is ever possible adequately to express in words the fundamentally inexpressible nature of God. Worship does not invariably require language: we can worship in corporate silence or through music. But although both silence and textless music can be a medium of worship, the liturgy – that shaped flow of the worshipping community's response in love and thankfulness to God – can only be articulated in words, inadequate as these may be. So we must at least attempt to arrive at certain principles which govern what those words should be and how they should be ordered.

Where does the search start? Behind text lies texture, the pattern of experience which has shaped the liturgy of the Church in England. The way in which this pattern has been built up is in many ways analogous to the way in which an English church building has developed and changed over the centuries, as successive generations have added to the structure, or rearranged the liturgical furnishings, or adapted parts of the building to uses very different from those initially envisaged in response to changing social and theological understandings of the Church and its proclamation.

In England, these layers of development are usually plain for anyone to see, with a mediaeval fabric bearing traces not only of the Reformation period, but frequently of the eighteenth century, if only in the wall monuments or light fittings, before undergoing a major 'restoration' at the hands of the Tractarians or their successors in the last century. In many churches the result is something which the radical purist finds rather muddled, but we tend to find endearing and describe as textured. The best of these churches are deeply satisfying because they articulate layers of experience, and illustrate Sir Ninian Comper's famous dictum of 'unity by inclusion'.

A rather different treatment has been meted out to many of the churches on the continent. In Italy, the fashion for 'de-baroquing' Romanesque churches has led to some remarkable successes and some grim, over-cleansed failures, while the ruthlessness of the restoration and reordering of some of the finest of the war-damaged churches in the Rhineland has produced some stunning interiors where nothing seems to have happened between the construction of the eleventh century and the furnishings of the present day!

These contrasting attitudes to the conservation of church buildings find a parallel in varying understandings of the nature of the Church which are evident today. Some models of the Church place greater weight on boundaries and belonging, and have as their focus an expressed doctrinal purity. In their search for uniformity, they can easily appear to be narrowly exclusive. Others uphold the principle of unity by inclusion, and value diversity as a sign of the rich variety of God's created order. They in turn can appear so indefinite in matters of belief that the pursuit of uncritical friendliness may appear to be prized above the truth.

While these patterns are properly understood as complementary, the bias in the Anglican tradition, for historical reasons connected with the Elizabethan Settlement, has tended towards the layered, inclusive approach. At the first sight, the one area in which this has not happened is the Church's worship. The distinctive place, enshrined in English law, given to the Book of Common Prayer in maintaining the worship and doctrine of the Church of England has not allowed for the natural and gradual evolution of forms of worship over the centuries, as is the case with church buildings, for example. And the Act of Uniformity continues to exert its pull to the extent that a parish priest has first to ask himself not what is the pastorally appropriate form for the liturgy to take, but what is the legal form allowed.

This lack of textual development through three centuries is at the heart of the Church's present dilemma, though the lack has not been as absolute as is sometimes imagined. For, at a second glance, one can see that forms of worship have evolved, even in matters of text as well as texture, though not often at the central points where change would be most significant.

In the first place, there are the layers of text in the liturgy which have grown up beyond the strict confines of the authorised order. Under the initial influence of Methodism, for example, robust hymnody has come to be accepted as a proper part of Anglican worship, as were the metrical psalms of Tate and Brady. And where would we be at Christmastide without the Festival of Nine Lessons and Carols devised by Bishop Benson for Truro Cathedral, or Eric Milner-White's Bidding Prayer made famous by King's College, Cambridge? It is by the words of well-known hymns and in rites such as these that religious consciousness is formed and memory sustained.

At the same time there are 'the customary deviations' which have regularly been made in the Prayer Book Order for Holy Communion – the omission of the long Exhortations, and even of the Collect for the Queen; the substitution of the Summary of the Law for the Ten Commandments; and the regular saying by the whole of the congregation of the prayer which represents that essentially private and personal strand in the liturgy – the Prayer of Humble Access – as if it were a corporate acclamation like the Gloria or even a general confession.

All these deviations and additions would be robustly defended by their practitioners as being within the spirit of the Prayer Book tradition. The pity is that the texts themselves bore such a weight doctrinally that they could never evolve naturally. The debacle over the Proposed Prayer Book in 1928 showed how far the gap between the authorised forms and actual practice had grown, and ensured that reform, when it came, would be more sharply accelerated than a gradual evolution would have allowed.

This has left us with a layered legacy of Prayer Book texts, eighteenth-century hymnody and its successors, nineteenth-century devotional writing and the liturgies of this century. Alongside this mainline track runs a literary tradition, with roots in the pre-Reformation vernacular as well as the popular late mediaeval Latin texts, from Lancelot Andrewes, George Herbert and John Bunyan down to T. S. Eliot and David Jones.

UNIFORMITY OF TEXT

Yet the impression remains for the ordinary worshipper that the Prayer Book tradition is a static one, and indeed some of those who most treasure it see that as part of its virtue. Though the truth may be more subtle and there may be more 'layering' even to the text of the liturgy than people recognise, the fact remains that development was not possible in the text of the liturgy in the period before 1967 in the same way that it was in, for instance, music or church architecture. The textual developments that did take place were more to do with what was excluded than what was created. It was almost inevitable that change should come in a sweeping away that seemed to some not far short of iconoclasm.

In a strange way it seems that part of the offence of the reforms that led to the Alternative Service Book was their very conservatism. A hesitant Liturgical Commission, and a more hesitant General Synod, preferred often to 'tinker' with long-established texts than to compose afresh. Better to modify Cranmer's Prayer of Humble Access, to iron out a doctrinal ambiguity and to make the language more contemporary, than to write a new prayer simply with echoes of the old to stand alongside it. So the Synod believed. It seemed a sane and sensitive approach, respectful to the tradition and moving worshippers on very gently. In retrospect it is easier to see that a better policy might have been to leave the old untampered, but to produce also new and creative material in a complementary but contemporary style, and to let the two exist side by side.

The Church of England still has a layered legacy, but recent layers have not always seemed to blend in with what was there before. There sometimes seems to be an inappropriate kind of dominance by the latest style that leaves every part of the furniture looking misplaced. How are things to be ordered in such a way that everything worthy has its place with an inclusiveness that achieves unity and harmony? And if the answer to that question could be found for a theoretical situation, can it be earthed in reality when the worship of the Church has to serve for so many different social and cultural constituencies?

Is it then to the texts or to the textures that we should look for the distinctive thread of Common Prayer in the Church of England today? If we are not afraid that counterpoint will undermine harmony, and can understand it to be mutually enriching, then a satisfying liturgy – though in a cathedral style – may well blend Byrd for Four Voices in

Latin with the celebrant's text from ASB Rite A, and readings from the RSV, accompanied by the Wesleys' hymns
and the congregation's spoken texts – the Creed and Our
Father, for example – in familiar BCP.

That will certainly provide a layered texture: what will
give it shape and direction? This is where the English
dramatic tradition has much to contribute. We need to be
able to articulate, by the way in which the liturgy is celebrated as much as anything, the distinction between plot
and sub-plot; between the major track of the dramatic
narrative, the light relief, or bystander's comment, and the
involvement of members of the audience, both as individuals and corporately. In those masterpieces of dramatic art,
the Bach Passions, this is precisely the way in which
different layers are assigned. The narrative belongs to the
Evangelist and other *personae dramatis,* including the crowd.
In the soloist's arias Bach provides the bystander's reflection,
and the use of familiar chorales, where the particular events
of one time and place are rooted in the Church's continuing
celebration of thanks and praise, offers to the congregation a
reassuring link with the regular worshipping tradition.

Drama also provides a sense of development and direction: plots unfold and random events take shape, characters
blossom into rounded people with whom we identify, and
an ordered pattern begins to emerge which catches us into
its momentum, so that at the end of the performance we
have been taken beyond where we had expected to be. Any
liturgy likewise reveals a deep pattern, of which we are
hardly conscious when we are caught up in its celebration.
But if we come to the end, and do not seem to have
advanced beyond our starting point, then we can legiti-
mately ask 'Where is it going?' Just as the root motive for
worship is the desire to offer all that we are to God in
thanksgiving for all that he has done for us, so the basic
vehicle is our entry into the prayer, the relationship, of the
Son to the Father. It is that movement Godwards which
provides direction and meaning to all that we are and do.

THE LANGUAGE OF LITURGY

How we clothe this essential movement in words which articulate it is the proper task of liturgical texts. They need to address the questions of where the liturgy is going, what is the socio-political context from which its elements have come and how do we translate them into our own cultural terms, and which images of the relationship between God and his people, between the Church and the kingdom, and between the divine promise and the human condition are valid in the context in which the worship will be offered.

Not that the texts are just texts, pure and simple. Texts are spoken and sung, they are proclamation and response, dialogue and reflection, texts for reading privately and for hearing publicly. And the texts imply more than the words on the page: they imply the text(ure) of the building and of the aural world; they imply the text(ure) of the participants – and not just the ministers – as they come together to provide the context of the celebration; and they are full of rubrics – the semi-suppressed indicators that this text is not primarily to be read but to be done. This reminder falls uncomfortably on some English ears, schooled in reading Shakespeare in the classroom and dissecting the play, rather than absorbing the drama from experiencing the play in the theatre. As has been said, 'In England they think first and do it afterwards; in Italy they do it first, and never think at all.'

But to say this is no excuse for the language not being intelligible to those who take part. Generally this means that simple words should be preferred to more complex, contemporary usage to archaic forms, the concrete to the nebulous, and that overwrought imagery should be eschewed. Beauty in language is achieved through the rhythm, strength and subtlety of the cadences and is not an adornment which can be tacked on like some decorative embellishment to an intrinsically graceless or unrhythmic building. But an emphasis on the virtues of intelligibility and simplicity can be dangerous if it results in a prose that is bland, pedestrian and unmemorable. We must not let our search for accessibility – a fashionable concern – result in a debased language which is neither modern nor traditional, and which can only too often be more appropriate to a school primer for beginners in English than to the worship of God.

The language should be able to stand the test of time without the need for constant revision. Words which are too contemporary in the sense that they embody fashionable linguistic concerns can very quickly become out of date, so that the liturgy, constantly rewritten and modernised, comes to reflect the restless need for change in contemporary life, rather than the eternal truths of the Christian gospel. Worshippers value the reassurance of familiar words, often hallowed by centuries of Christian use. It can be argued that the language of worship can never be totally contemporary, since it is concerned with the spiritual and the eternal.

Nevertheless the Church is presented today with a particular challenge. Liturgy in England has not been constantly rewritten and modernised. As we have seen, in terms of official liturgical text, it had until a generation ago been left almost untouched for generations. Rewriting and modernising has so far been the activity of little more than a generation. It is not reasonable to expect the 'first drafts', so to speak, of our liturgical writers, especially when their art has had so little scope for development in the past, to be deeply satisfying and instantly acceptable. The Church has to accept that a creative process, however sensitively undertaken, will involve both error and pain, and a certain amount of tearing up and beginning again. At one level a new liturgical style cannot be sought – literature simply does not happen like that. It is too artificial an exercise to set out to create the memorable. But, equally, the wordsmiths need space to grow more confident and subtle in their art, and the Church must be prepared to search with them for the finest contemporary material to stand alongside the time-hallowed texts of earlier generations.

Liturgical language, even newly composed texts, must always live close to the danger of belonging to the past. Texts composed for particular occasions may be intentionally striking or even strident, but texts for regular use week by week need to be capable of public recitation, memorable and memorised, and even new texts will inevitably draw on older phrases and images. Part of what worshippers do in employing liturgical words, rooted in the Church's tradition, is to *remember,* and to remember is something much more theologically significant than simply reciting a text known by heart. The petition to the General Synod in the *PN Review* in 1979 spoke of 'this great act of forgetting, now under way [which] is a tragic loss to our historic memory and an impoverishment of present awareness'. Without the King James Bible and the Book of Common Prayer, it argued, 'the resources of expression are reduced, the stock of shared words depleted, and we ourselves diminished'. It is this last point that must most concern the Church. When Christians no longer remember, when, in the petition's striking phrase, they share in a 'great act of forgetting', they are diminished. There is a sense in which it is not only the individual Christian who is diminished, but in the loss of corporate memory Church and nation are diminished.

Yet, at a more simple level, the remembering of individual Christians is crucial. If people's souls are to be fed, they need to have deep within them words committed to memory, that can surface in time of need, supremely in time of mortal illness and approaching death. The danger is that both the quality of some of our modern liturgical writing, and even the sheer variety of it, mean that generations are growing up that have no texts, new or old, in their memory to feed their souls. Some will see in this a strong argument for a return to Prayer Book texts, and, even more, to the Authorised Version of the Bible. Others will argue for more contemporary forms of both service book and Bible, but richer and more rhythmic in style than much of what is now on offer, and, crucially, for a whole-hearted adoption of them and an end to the period of experiment with core liturgical texts. Whether with the old words alone, or, as the majority of churchpeople probably favour, with old and new together, it is now time for assimilation.

The Church has seemed slow to recognise the foolishness of a 'great act of forgetting', though, in truth, it is only twenty-five years since the process of liturgical reform began. It is not too late to recover a sense of continuity and to resolve to live in a Church with a layered liturgy. The danger that must be guarded against now, in taking this on board, is that of returning to an approach where liturgy can fossilise. History has taught us that that can only lead eventually to iconoclasm. If we are to remember, we must also remember the lesson of recent years, and encourage the liturgists in each generation to go on adding quietly to the riches of our worship the very best they can give us to help us draw close to God.

PHYLLIS JAMES
MICHAEL PERHAM
DAVID STANCLIFFE

5

The Liturgy In Its Social Context

LITURGY SHAPED IN TIME OF TURMOIL

The almost timeless beauty of the language and form of the Book of Common Prayer, together with the way it carefully holds to the balances of Anglicanism, provide some of the clues to its durability. It is quite extraordinary that a book of liturgy should have survived over such a long period in the life of a Church and become so much part of what that Church is all about.

There are, I believe, other reasons for its longevity, which I have not the skill to explore in depth but which are worthy of serious consideration. These reasons are to do with the Prayer Book's understanding of the place and role of the Church in England. These matters may help in the contemporary task of forming liturgies to serve the worship of the Church today.

The study of modern liturgies from other parts of the world helps us to see the importance of this perspective. The new South African Prayer Book is clearly affected by the traumas of the struggle to throw off apartheid. Its mood, language and particular prayers are all framed with this background in mind. The theological thrust of the book is made in response to the living mission of a Church set in this difficult situation.

This, for example, is part of the Fourth Eucharistic Prayer in the South African Prayer Book:[1]

> By the power of the Holy Spirit he took flesh of the Virgin Mary and shared our human nature. He lived and died as one of us, to reconcile us to you, the God and Father of all.

> In fulfilment of your will he stretched out his hands in
> suffering, to bring release to those who place their hope in
> you; and so won for you a holy people.
>
> He chose to bear our griefs and sorrows, and to give up his life
> on the cross, that he might shatter the chains of the evil one,
> and banish the darkness of sin and death. (p. 125)

Key words and phrases pick up the life of the people: 'one
of us', 'reconcile', 'suffering', 'release', 'hope', 'griefs and
sorrows', 'the chains', 'the darkness'. Similarly the Prayers
for the World (pp. 86f) pick up the experience of a nation
in the midst of struggle for justice and peace.

The Book of Common Prayer was similarly shaped in
the midst of religious and political controversy. It was affected by the Reformation and the desire to sever the links
with Rome. It developed in the struggle for the meaning of
Protestantism in England, which was brought to a head by
the growth of the Puritan movement, and which was settled
in the outcome of the battle between Crown and Commonwealth in the seventeenth century. Although, sadly, the
outcome of all this was not a united Church in the nation,
embracing the whole Christian family, it did lead to a
Prayer Book which struck some important notes and
balances in its understanding of Church and nation.

First, the Prayer Book is committed to the concept of a
national Church, holding to the catholic faith and to the
essential structure of catholic order. Thus it both rejects the
authority of Rome over the Church in this land and affirms
that the Church of England remains part of the one holy
catholic Church. It recognises the right of the Crown in
Parliament to provide laws for the government of the
Church and assumes that both Crown and Parliament
accept some sort of allegiance to the Church for which they
hold responsibilities. Richard Hooker's vision of the one
society, of which the institutions of both Church and State
are different but integral faces, is not far off the way the
Prayer Book views things.

Secondly, it is committed to the idea that this nation accepts itself as a Christian nation and that this is expressed in the nation's commitment to the Church. The Church of England is the Church of all the people of the nation.[2] Its worship is therefore for all the people of the nation. If on the one hand it rejects Roman interference, on the other it rejects Anabaptist and sectarian options. The Church is not a gathered congregation, apart from the community. It is the place within which the Christian faith is set forth in word and sacrament, inviting all the people to come, hear and participate. The place of the Church in society, under the Crown, is symbolic of a commitment by this society consciously to understand itself as Christian.

The liturgy needs therefore to be accessible to a much wider range of people than those who are habitual worshippers. The language should be simple (though not superficial), the rubrics clear and easy to understand, and, in an age of great mobility, the liturgy ought to be recognisable across the Church as a whole. Again, the South African Prayer Book has some useful examples. Its Baptism service begins with a welcome and a simple statement about the meaning of the rite. The ASB, in contrast, begins with a list of duties for parents and godparents. The renunciation in the South African service is tougher and earthed in their experience. The rubrics of their service are set out clearly.

Thirdly, the Prayer Book is committed to the supremacy of the Crown, but not to any dogma such as the 'divine right of kings'. Its view of the place of the Crown is practical rather than ideological. The Crown is the focus of the unity of the nation, and as such carries responsibilities for the Church. Thus the Prayer Book, and with it the seventeenth-century settlement, rode the middle way between Stuart ideas of the divine right of kings and Puritan notions of commonwealth. Anglicanism has continued to hold to this practical view of power.

Fourthly, the Church, as the trustee of the gospel within the nation, and as the body with responsibility for the spiritual welfare of the nation, should help in the provision of charity and care for those in need. Not only does it provide common worship and basic Christian education, it also cares for the poor.

These themes can all be found in the Book of Common Prayer. That book was honed in a context where theological, ecclesiastical and political conflicts were intertwined. It is rooted in the Reformation and the peculiarly English and Anglican understanding of the reform of the Church.

PRAYER BOOK LESSONS IN TODAY'S CULTURE

The outcome, although by no means settling in a united Church serving one nation, carried sufficient commitment within the nation to express where many thought both Church and nation ought to be. The Prayer Book view of the place and role of the Church in the community has embedded itself in the culture of this nation. It has not been until the twentieth century that a severe, and possibly even terminal, weakening of this aspect of our culture has come about. It has been in this same century that the move to provide other liturgies has grown and taken hold on the life of the Church. One cannot avoid asking whether the two are connected.

This is a very difficult time to be attempting liturgical reform, because it is not at all clear whether we need simply to adjust the Prayer Book understanding of the role of the Church or to replace it with something else. No satisfactory liturgy for the Church can be provided until that issue is addressed. *The Alternative Service Book 1980* may be a useful beginning to permanent liturgical reform. It cannot rest there, not just because its language is dull (which it is) or sexist (which it is much more so than the Book of Common Prayer, and without good reason), but also because it has no conscious idea of what understanding of the place and mission of the Church it is trying to sustain. The book is tempted into echoing the predominant culture of the age in its more superficial elements, rather than discovering the deeper roots of spirituality in this community.

This may be a harsh judgement. It is not meant as such, because the ASB has started us on a road that has to be trod. Its transient nature, however, is rooted in a number of unresolved issues which are not just liturgical matters in isolation, or indeed matters of pure theology. They are matters to do with what the Church of England believes needs to be planted and developed in this society both now and into the future.

DEVELOPING THE TRADITION

I would suggest that we need to develop the tradition represented in the Book of Common Prayer, rather than seem to replace it. Inevitably different people will see a variety of directions in which that development should take place. My own rather preliminary thoughts go in the following direction.

First, we should affirm the continuing need to express the duty of the Church to provide worship, education, pastoral care and compassionate action for all without discrimination. We should continue to reject sectarian options or, more important for Anglicanism in this country, congregational denominationalism. This is a task, in an ecumenical age, which must be sensitively shared with all Christians who want to participate in it. The Church of England is a custodian of its inheritance on behalf of all.

To take one example, the Prayers and Thanksgivings of the 1928 Prayer Book (and to some extent of the 1662 Book of Common Prayer) are of much greater range and much nearer to the daily life of the whole community than the meagre fare of the ASB Prayers for Various Occasions. Government and citizenship, work and leisure, domestic life, poverty and plenty, war and peace, education and understanding, are all matters which a prayer book should include. If these prayers ring true to the life of the community and are in a language that people can internalise, they can grow into the culture.

Secondly, we need to affirm the concept of political power. In the Book of Common Prayer this attaches to the Crown, but can be made to include democratic institutions at all levels. Respect and honour for the institutions which give shape to our society should not, of course, lapse into a baptism of what they may stand for or do at any one time.

Thirdly, we need to underline an understanding of the 'establishment of the Church' that emphasises the Christian nature of our society, rather than any concept of privilege for the Church. The 'establishment' is not to be bound to any particular process for the appointment of bishops, but to a continuing sense of this nation holding on to, and indeed reviving, its Christian inheritance. When that is understood in open and welcoming terms, it poses no threat to those in our society who hold to other faiths or to none. Pluralism does not in practice have to end up as a society having no fundamental commitments that express its history and its ethics. Anglicanism is, in its gut, an inclusive part of the Christian inheritance. Inclusiveness does not have to undermine its distinctiveness as part of the catholic Church.

Liturgy should be able to embrace a wide range of people present at its celebration. People of other faiths and of none ought not to be embarrassed by the worship of the Church. There are important occasions when people from many backgrounds will be present: occasional offices, civic occasions and community-based events. The presentation and experience of Christian worship can serve to draw into its heart the spiritual longings of many. Some of the material in books such as *The Promise of His Glory,* when used with movement, music and colour, can impart the challenge and the welcome of the gospel without undermining the integrity of those who do not call themselves Christians. Worship flows from the gift of God, not the faith of the people. It can evoke and create faith in all who come within its orbit.

These somewhat jumbled thoughts, if they have anything of value, do affect the detail of liturgical work. This is especially important in a church which expresses its convictions through its books of worship. Thus the mood of the liturgy, the content of its prayers, readings and rubrics, its language and style, all have to be considered against this background. How are we to help the people of this nation to worship, to shape their lives and this community by such prayer, and to help provide that context of spiritual life and experience which can help sustain the institutions and culture of our community? These are questions and issues which liturgical innovators should have running through their own spiritual bloodstream.

JOHN GLADWIN

NOTES

[1] *An Anglican Prayer Book 1989:* Church of the Province of Southern Africa (Collins 1989).

[2] Rowan Williams makes a similar plea for an open and inclusive understanding of the Church in his essay 'Imagining the Kingdom' in Kenneth Stevenson and Bryan Spinks (eds.), *The Identity of Anglican Worship* (Mowbray: London 1991), pp. 1-13.

6

An Ecumenical Approach to
Common Prayer

COMMON PRAYER AND ENGLISH
NONCONFORMITY

If commonality in prayer is to be judged according to the standard of the Book of Common Prayer, then for many generations there has been a significant proportion of worshipping Christians in England who, on any Sunday, have failed to come up to that standard. Only Anglicans who have allowed themselves to be carefully and completely isolated from all the other Christians traditions with which we are surrounded can imagine that there are no other styles and traditions of worship other than that with which the Church of England has been associated. Indeed, it is a matter of sad, but historical, fact that the Book of Common Prayer has been used at various times as a religious test, a shibboleth which was capable of rooting out the deviant, a means of discovering those who were not, as the Preface describes them, 'sober, peaceable, and truly conscientious sons of the Church of England'. Often this was in order that the penalties of non-conformity might be duly administered.

Thus 'common prayer' was a concept to which, until quite recently, only members of the Church of England subscribed and which others had reason to fear or even to despise. Some English Christians were content, indeed keen, to follow other ways. In the first place, from the mid-seventeenth century many of the Puritans and Separatists were highly suspicious of the Book of Common Prayer because of the large measure of continuity it obviously had with the Roman Catholic past. It has been said that

> The Prayer Book had been compiled using the old Latin rites as a basis, and these had been made scriptural as far as the Royal authority deemed it necessary.[1]

Therefore, for the Puritans and Separatists it was necessary either to adapt the Prayer Book or to use rites derived from those Reformed Churches who had more comprehensively purified their worship. Later the Independents, in their turn, had little time for liturgical forms, and it was not until the nineteenth century, by which time they were known as Congregationalists, that they began to take any interest in liturgical worship.[2]

In contrast to this, which might be called 'classical' liturgical nonconformity, the Methodist tradition was initially more Prayer Book-based. Certainly Charles Wesley had a great love for the Book of Common Prayer and used it regularly when conducting public worship, even after he no longer held any official post within the Church of England. In a sermon from that time, he said: 'I hold all the doctrines of the Church of England. I love her liturgy'.[3] The Countess of Huntingdon's Connexion, which was an attempt to make Methodism acceptable to the genteel, used the Prayer Book at its services. However, two traditions emerged within Methodism: one which kept close to Anglican models and another which was free of prescribed forms of prayer and orders of service. Even so, there was an increasing tendency for the free form of service to supplant the other, even if this was not necessarily the wish of the Methodist Conference. As early as 1795 the Conference had laid down that

> Wherever Divine service is performed in England on the Lord's Day in Church-hours the officiating preacher shall read either the service of the Established Church, our venerable father's abridgement, or, at least the lessons appointed by the Calendar. But we recommend either the full service, or the abridgement.[4]

45

It is certainly true that the Methodist celebration of the Lord's Supper was the Prayer Book service with only relatively minor amendments. Yet it did have certain very definite features, especially through its intrinsic connections with an evangelical revival.[5] The first of these was to have an enormous influence upon Anglican worship and also to provide perhaps the most 'common' feature of all Christian worship in England. This was hymnody. By their introduction of hymnody into the Prayer Book service the Wesleys were trying to revive an ancient Christian tradition which required that the supreme act of Christian worship needed the element of singing for its fullest expression.[6]

Hymn-singing was opposed by the earliest Tractarians, who were their own particular kind of Prayer Book fundamentalists. At what might be called the inaugural meeting of the Oxford Movement, held at Hadleigh in July 1833, it was resolved to defend 'the apostolical succession and the integrity of the Prayer Book'. They were anxious to recall the Church to the full and proper use of the Prayer Book and a strict interpretation of its rubrics. Indeed, Isaac Williams was bold enough to entitle Tract 86, which came from his pen, 'Indications of a Superintending Providence in the Preservation of the Prayer Book and in the changes which it has undergone'. The novelties in both text and ceremony were to be a feature of later stages of the Oxford Movement, not of its concerns and preoccupations in the 1830s and '40s. Hymn-singing was nowhere mentioned in the Prayer Book (with the solitary exception of the Ordinal); therefore it was not to be encouraged.

Nonetheless it eventually became a much-loved ingredient in all forms of worship. It can, with confidence, be claimed that Methodism, and the Free Churches in general, have given to worship in England its most pervasive and significant common feature, one which was never envisaged by the Prayer Book compilers. Anglicans have been slow to learn the best way of using hymns in worship. Too often they are used as no more than musical interludes. Nevertheless, the average worshipper in any church would take the presence of hymns in any act of worship as a *sine qua non*.

A second significant feature of Free Church worship has only recently found its place in Anglican worship, but is now firmly established. That is the use of extempore prayer. It was not until the Alternative Service Book that those who conducted Anglican worship had any encouragement to pray in their own words, so hedged around were Anglicans by the use of 'the Book'.

OTHER BRITISH TRADITIONS

Up to now we have only been considering the common elements as they exist in worship in England, but it ought not to be forgotten that there are other models worthy of consideration within the United Kingdom. In December 1562 the General Assembly of the Church of Scotland officially replaced the 1552 Prayer Book, so far as the Communion went, by the Book of Common Order (or the Order of Geneva).

The Book of Common Order was not strictly a liturgy, rather was it a guide to public worship for ministers and readers. Its use was not to be fixed and obligatory, although the officiating minister was clearly not meant to depart from, or vary too much, the actual form of words. He was not to be guided merely by his own predilections.

> It is not the tradition of the Reformed Church of Scotland to leave the framing of its public prayers to the ideas, prejudices, or eccentricities of the Ministers.[7]

Even so, there was a great deal of scope for personal choice and decision by the Minister, and this element was maintained in the subsequent liturgical history of the Church of Scotland, even when the original Book of Common Order had ceased to be authorised and other traditions had been established.[8]

'Common prayer' would seem to be an ideal sought after by the English – certainly the Churches of the Welsh revival knew nothing of it – and even then, principally, it was the preoccupation of one particular Church, the Church of England. Eventually the other Churches developed an interest in liturgical matters, but this was not until the nineteenth century.[9] Even then they did so, not in order to use liturgical forms as any kind of trial or test, but out of convictions which were based upon both good scholarship and perceived pastoral needs and necessities.

For over fifty years now it has been realised, by those interested in the Ecumenical Movement, that seeking to enter into an understanding of one another's ways of worship might be a highly practical means of removing some of those obstacles to unity which arise out of differences in faith and order. Consequently attempts were made at different levels among the churches to commence this task which, it was realised, was one of both education and self-revelation.[10] It was soon discovered that nearly all the Western Churches had been affected by some kind of 'liturgical movement'. The Liturgical Movement, as a whole, can be described as a recovery by the Church of an understanding that its worship is central to its life and its work. The term was used in the first place to describe the work done in continental Europe by Roman Catholic scholars and pastors to remove the accretions of the past and to restore the celebration of the liturgy to the whole people of God. Yet it was more than just tinkering with texts or ceremonial, it had a deeper theological *raison d'être*. As Robert L. Tuzik has recently written:

> The European leaders of the liturgical movement set out to do more than move furniture and have people sing chants at Mass. They wanted to reform the way people lived as church. They came to understand the liturgy as a celebration of what it means to be, to become and to build up the church. They wanted to rescue popular piety from its preoccupation with worship before the tabernacle to a style of worship that would relate the liturgy to life. They wanted the liturgy to become

the source of life of the church, the source of the lay aposto-late.[11]

Not all the Churches were directly affected by what the Roman Catholic Church was doing, but the results were remarkably similar, regardless of the individual Church's starting point.[12] The common realisation, it was discovered, was the need to place the Eucharist at the very centre of the worship-life of the Church; to see it as the summation of all Christian worship and the definitive link between the corporate life of the Church and the life of the world in which the Church is set. And the second shared realisation was that the eucharistic action must be both accessible and understandable to all worshippers.

ECUMENICAL LITURGICAL CO-OPERATION IN BRITAIN

In 1963, at the invitation of the then Archbishop of Canterbury (Michael Ramsey) liturgists from all the main-stream Churches in Great Britain came together to form the Joint Liturgical Group (JLG) under the chairmanship of a historian of the Book of Common Prayer, Douglas Harrison, the Dean of Bristol.[13] The Group has produced a series of books which have made a contribution to the revision of the service books of all the British Churches and in many other places in the world. The first book, however, was a series of essays in contemporary understanding of worship and liturgy particularly as they have been influenced by the various Liturgical Movements which we have noted.[14] Thereafter, the books were more practical: on the Calendar and Lectionary, the Daily Office, and the liturgical observance of Holy Week. The influence of each of these can be clearly seen in *The Alternative Service Book 1980* and in *The Book of Common Order* (1979).

The JLG was thus well placed to represent the British Churches in a further creative stage of ecumenical liturgical co-operation.

ECUMENICAL PRAYERS IN COMMON

In the van of the new dawn of liturgical awareness and adventure, which was inaugurated by the Liturgical Movement, was the Roman Catholic Church, and there is little need here to chronicle the details of its development in that Church.[15] It came to a climax with the promulgation of the Second Vatican Council's Constitution on the Liturgy, *Sacrosanctum Concilium,* in 1963. One of the effects of implementation of the Constitution was the realisation of the need for liturgical texts in the vernacular so that both the liturgical words and actions were indeed 'accessible and understandable to the worshipper'.

The fact that the Vatican issued an invitation for six ecumenical observers to be present during all meetings of the Concilium might have given a clue to subsequent developments.[16] In 1962 the Roman Catholic Church set up an 'English Liturgical Committee', just before the completion of the work on the Constitution on the Liturgy. It was this committee which was to become the International Commission on English in Liturgy (ICEL). ICEL, from the first, has represented thirty (Roman Catholic) Episcopal Conferences in English-speaking nations around the world. But it was agreed by those Episcopal Conferences, in the formal mandate which it gave to ICEL, that its work of 'achieving an English version of liturgical texts acceptable to English-speaking countries' was to be done 'bearing in mind the ecumenical aspects'.[17]

The outcome of this decision was that ICEL was instrumental in developing a specifically ecumenical liturgical body: the International Consultation on English Texts (ICET). From the beginning the British Churches were represented on it by JLG. The formation of ICET was a conscious decision made by the Roman Catholic Church that its search for contemporary vernacular texts would not be undertaken in isolation, but in co-operation with the other major English-speaking denominations throughout the world. The result was the drafting, by ICET, of texts such as Nicene Creed, Gloria in Excelsis, Sursum Corda, Sanctus, Benedictus for the Eucharist, as well as a series of canticles for use in the Office. Each of these were texts which had always belonged to the whole Church, and could not be thought of as being the property of any particular part of it, as their personal possession. The 1970 report which contained the texts made the point forcibly by its title, *Prayers We Have in Common*. They are now an integral part of the Service Books of many denominations throughout the English-speaking world.

Here then is a new and exciting aspect of Common Prayer. Prayers which are actively shared across the denominations, as well as across the nations. These texts serve as a liturgical and textual *lingua franca* in any country where English is spoken. This achieves a degree of commonality which hitherto would have been quite unimaginable.

In recent years ICET has been refounded. It has looked again at *Prayers We Have in Common* and has recently published a light revision which takes into consideration current sensitivity regarding the subject of 'inclusive language'.[18] But in order that its brief might be seen to include a wider range of liturgical matters which are of common concern than merely texts, and, incidentally, to avoid some of the previous confusion with ICEL, it is now known as the English Language Liturgical Consultation (ELLC). ELLC, among other tasks, is currently involved in the composition of a lectionary which will enable divided Christians to share the same biblical lections at their respective Sunday worship. While it is still sadly a fact that many of the Churches are separated at the Lord's Table, some compensation can be gained from the realisation that we can be united in the reading and exposition of the scriptures at our Sunday worship. This too we can have in common.[19]

Meanwhile the Roman Catholic ICEL is actively engaged in the massive programme of revising *The Roman Missal*. A series of progress reports have already been circulated and ICEL has stated that it has every confidence that it will be able to issue the proposed revised texts of the Missal in June 1994, in order that they can be carefully considered by the world-wide Episcopal Conferences.[20]

This impressive piece of work will need to be studied with equal care by the other Churches. At all stages, the Roman Catholic Church has made available to the Churches its revision proposals. Although ICEL only represents the English-speaking nations, it is in close touch with similar commissions and consultations which exist in other parts of the world, not least in Europe, and, of course, with the Congregation for Divine Worship and the Discipline of the Sacraments in Rome.

A NEW CONCEPT OF COMMON PRAYER

Sometimes we are tempted to be dismissive when either a non-Roman Catholic on holiday in Europe goes to Mass or, perhaps, a Roman Catholic, finding himself at an Anglican Eucharist, says, 'It is *so* similar'. One of the most satisfactory of the results of the various liturgical movements throughout the churches is the acceptance of a more or less common shape. Even if the language is unfamiliar, we can see and know where we are up to in the service. This is equally true when worshipping in many Free Church situations. There is a European common liturgical market in which we must rejoice.

It is essential that we build on this important gain in understanding. We will do this best, not only by each individual Church supporting ecumenical enterprises such as the Joint Liturgical Group and ELLC, but also by making sure that we carefully study each other's developing ideas and actively share our expertise. Recognition of our common liturgical roots and ecumenically agreed texts do not necessarily lead to convergence and agreement, yet it is a fact that there is now more 'in common' across the denominational boundaries than there ever has been since the divisions of the sixteenth century. This must mean that liturgical revision is, as it was hoped, making a significant and positive contribution to the day when, like the early apostles, we will indeed be able to break bread together and have all things in common.

DONALD GRAY

NOTES

[1] Bryan D. Spinks, *From the Lord and 'The Best Reformed Churches': A Study of the Eucharistic Theology in the English Puritan and Separatist Traditions, 1556-1633* (Rome 1984), p. 22.

[2] Bryan D. Spinks, *Freedom or Order: The Eucharist-Liturgy in English Congregationalism 1645-1980* (Allison Park, Pennsylvania, 1984), pp. 20ff.

[3] Sermon CXV, 'The Ministerial Office', in T. Jackson (ed.), *Wesley's Works*, 11th edn (London 1856), vol. VII, p. 266.

[4] Rupert Davies, A. Raymond George, Gordon Rupp (eds.), *A History of the Methodist Church in Great Britain* (London 1965-83), vol. 2, p. 124.

[5] Trevor Dearing, *Wesleyan and Tractarian Worship* (London 1966), pp. 12-13.

[6] Though it is the Baptists who can probably claim to be the pioneers in the introduction of congregational hymn-singing in England. E. G. Rupp, *Religion in England 1688-1791* (Oxford 1986), p. 131.

[7] George B. Burnet, *The Holy Communion in the Reformed Church of Scotland, 1560-1960* (Edinburgh 1960), p. 12.

[8] James F. White, *Protestant Worship: Traditions in Transition* (Louisville, Kentucky, 1989), pp. 72-3.

[9] Spinks, *Freedom or Order*, op. cit., pp. 87ff; N. P. Goldhawk, 'The Methodist People in the Early Victorian Age: Spirituality and Worship', in Davies, George, Rupp, op. cit., pp. 113ff; Burnet, op. cit., pp. 265ff.

[10] The beginnings of this work can be seen in Peter Edwall, Eric Hayman, William D. Maxwell (eds.), *Ways of Worship: The Report of a Theological Commission of Faith and Order* (London 1951), *passim*, while Max Thurian (ed.) *Ecumenical Perspectives on Baptism, Eucharist and Ministry*, Faith and Order Paper 116 (Geneva 1983) shows how far the Churches have moved since then.

[11] Robert L. Tuzik (compiler), *How Firm a Foundation: Leaders of the Liturgical Movement* (Chicago 1990), p.4.

[12] Michael J. Taylor, *The Protestant Liturgical Renewal: A Catholic Viewpoint* (Westminster, Maryland, 1963), *passim*.

[13] D. E. W. Harrison, *The Book of Common Prayer: The Anglican Heritage of Public Worship* (London and Edinburgh 1946).

[14] Ronald C. D. Jasper (ed.), *The Renewal of Worship: Essays by Members of the Joint Liturgical Group* (Oxford 1965).

[15] For a personalised, but accurate, account see Bernard Botte (tr. John Sullivan OCD), *From Silence to Participation: An Insider's View of Liturgical Renewal* (Washington DC 1988).

[16] Annibale Bugnini (tr. Matthew J. O'Connell), *The Reform of the Liturgy 1948-1975* (Collegeville, Minnesota, 1990), p. 200.

[17] See Peter C. Finn and James M. Schellmann (eds.), *Shaping English Liturgy* (Washington DC 1990), pp. 433ff.

[18] *Praying Together,* English Language Liturgical Consultation (London and Nashville, Tennessee, 1988).

[19] *The Revised Common Lectionary,* Consultation on Common Texts (London, Winfield BC and Nashville, Tennessee, 1992).

[20] *Third Progress Report on the Revision of the Roman Missal* (ICEL, Washington DC 1992).

7

Not So Common Prayer:
The Third Service

NO REAL UNIFORMITY

In 1872 the Act of Uniformity Amendment Act was passed which amongst other things allowed a 'Third Service' on Sundays as a supplement to the statutory services of Morning and Evening Prayer provided in the Prayer Book.[1] Although in terms of legality this was a new provision, it is important to understand that it was making legal something which in various guises had existed in the Church of England from the sixteenth century. Indeed, the idea that the Church of England ever had complete liturgical uniformity as provided by the services in the Book of Common Prayer is simply not true. In the Elizabethan Church the Prayer Book had been supplemented by the Primers, which provided an alternative and more varied form of Office for private and informal use.[2] At the same time many Puritan clergy adapted and changed the Prayer Book services by adding and omitting material, often 'Presbyterianizing' the services.[3] Any belief that the Restoration Church with a new Act of Uniformity fared any better has been shattered by the recent study of John Spurr.[4] Not only did some clergy still refuse to wear the surplice, but there were still instances of clergy emending and shortening the statutory services. Part of the problem (but only part) was the custom of running together Morning Prayer, the Litany and Ante-Communion, which was not only interminably long, but also involved considerable repetition. Already in the Liturgy of Comprehension of 1689 (an attempt to bring in the moderate Presbyterians) provision was discussed for creating two or three separate services by rearranging the material of those services. It must also be remembered that other occasional and informal services existed. Throughout the later sixteenth and for most of the seventeenth century special services were drawn up in times of disaster, using cento psalmody.[5] Also, the practice of catechizing children in the afternoon tended to attract some prayers, making it semi-liturgical.

THE NINETEENTH CENTURY: THE IMMEDIATE CONTEXT

By the nineteenth century the need for more flexibility was keenly felt, not least by clergy who did not want to repeat Evensong at a later hour for servants unable to attend earlier services. After the Religious Census of 1851 a Joint Committee was appointed in 1854 to consider if any changes in the rules of worship were needed. It reported in the July of that year and advocated permission for occasional services compiled from Prayer Book materials.[6] Already there were some attempts to reach the 'unchurched millions' which the Census had revealed, and a number of Evangelical clergy engaged in open-air preaching services. In 1855 Lord Shaftesbury managed to get a modification of the law which prohibited meetings for worship of more than twenty people in any building except a church or a licensed dissenting chapel. In the same year simple Sunday evening services were held for the non-churchgoer in Exeter Hall, London, and later seven theatres in the poorer parts of London were rented and the special 'informal' worship held in these buildings met with immediate success.[7] In Portsmouth the Evangelical incumbent of St. John's, Portsea, acquired the use of a former circus building in 1857 in which experimental services were held for the benefit of working people:

after singing two verses of the National Anthem, the more instructive and generally interesting portions of the newspapers are read... A hymn is then sung, and a prayer offered... The meeting concludes with the doxology.[8]

During the 1861 revival, William Pennefather, the vicar of Christ Church, Barnet, held a series of informal evening mission services which consisted mainly of preaching and prayer. These led to extemporising in the General Thanksgiving on Sundays.[9]

However, there appears to have been conflicting views regarding what was actually needed and for whom. In *Suggestions for the Preparation of a Third Service for use on Sundays Between Morning and Evening Prayer,* 1869, the Rev. Lord Alwyne Compton wrote:

It was said that we require a new service suitable for use to an ignorant, possibly a half-heathen, congregation in large towns; to those who are not yet regular church-goers. For this purpose considerable freedom should be left to the minister.[10]

Compton's own proposals, however, were not concerned with what had come to be called 'bridge services' or missionary services. He was concerned for a form which was 'suited to the same classes of persons as attend the afternoon or evening service now, who might perhaps have a difficulty in following, or be offended by the peculiarities of any thing very new to them'.[11] He proposed ransacking the ancient medieval Offices for material, and appealed to Archdeacon Freeman's *Principles of Divine Service*.

Non-statutory services were not just the preserve of Evangelicals. Although some Anglo-Catholics favoured Compline with variable lessons as a regular 'Third Service',[12] in 'mission' contexts informal services were required. For the 1869 mission, *The Book of the Mission* had an evening service which included the Lord's Prayer, lesson, Psalms 51 and 120 and collects, as well as the sermon. It also contained a form of renewal of baptismal vows, using material from the communion, baptismal and confirmation services.[13]

As a result of the growing ritual controversy as well as these experiments with non-Prayer Book forms, a Royal Commission on Ritual was appointed in 1867. Its Fourth Report of 1870 made certain proposals which were incorporated into the 1872 Act.

THE PROVISIONS OF THE 1872 ACT

The 1872 Act (18 July) dealt with a number of issues, including, for example, shortening Morning and Evening Prayer (but in a cathedral or collegiate church, only in addition to the full services!) and allowing the Litany to be used after Evensong. Regarding the 'Third Service', the Act allowed special services for special occasions, approved by the ordinary, and containing nothing, except anthems and hymns, which does not form part of the Scriptures or Book of Common Prayer. It also allowed an additional service varying from any form prescribed in the Prayer Book at any hour on a Sunday, provided that Morning Prayer, Evensong and Ante-Communion are read on the same day at another hour. Apart from the hymns and anthems, the material must come from Scripture and the Prayer Book – though not from Holy Communion. Its form, then, was to be left to the incumbent, acting under the authority of his bishop.

Whatever the intentions of the Act, its provisions were regarded by many as too timid, or clergy were unaware of how to use them. An anonymous author writing in 1876/7 complained:

> It is clearly unpractical to offer home or foreign pagans the refined and intellectual Book of Common Prayer, and it only, as their guide and manual of devotion. The mere mechanical difficulty of finding the places is enough to baffle most of them, without the additional perplexity of trying to understand the matter when found. Some more elementary, simply constructed, and flexible offices, or skeletons of offices, permitting almost any degree of modification, seem needful for wants of such classes, for whom the Mission-room must serve as the porch and school of the Church, just as the scattered syna-

gogues of ancient Palestine were employed to train the Jews
with familiarity with the liturgical system of the central Temple
at Jerusalem.[14]

The writer complained that intercession, dedication and
thanksgiving were poorly provided for by the Prayer Book.
His complaint, shorn of its patronising attitude to 'home
pagans', is not too dissimilar to the complaints heard even in
the 1980s. Perhaps it was this type of complaint which led
the Convocations in 1892 to allow the use of material
which was substantially in agreement with Scripture and the
Prayer Book, thus widening the resources that could be
used. In fact the 1872 Act, together with the 1892 Convocations agreement, has meant that any service which is
consonant with the teaching of Scripture and the Prayer
Book is legal, provided that it is in addition to and not a
replacement of the statutory services. The problem which
arose in the twentieth century is that this type of service has
replaced the authorised forms.

Another catalyst for informal worship, growing out of
catechism, was the nineteenth-century Sunday School
movement, which often involved worship including
collects, prayers and intercession, Bible reading and hymns.
With a sizeable group and when celebrated in Church this
was a type of 'Third Service' with an emphasis on children.

It was also recognised that in 'mission' contexts other
forms of worship were necessary. For the London Mission
of 1874, the opening service which was held at St Paul's
was a special compilation, and at St Thomas, Regent Street,
the clerical journalist C. M. Davies described a Mission
service which included a metrical litany ('It was a bright,
sparkling composition in six-eight time, very effective and
appropriate',[15] collects, Psalm 51 sung to Gregorian chant,
and hymns. And the great Father Dolling held regular
mission services, which he described as 'our little Dissenting
services'. These consisted of hymns, a very informal talk,
and extempore prayer with 'hearty amens' interspersed by
many of the congregation.[16]

THE TWENTIETH-CENTURY FAMILY SERVICE

Three concerns have been encountered so far: desire for flexibility and enrichment; need for modification for those who are fringers; and children's worship. This trinity of concerns have formed the core of the twentieth-century Family Services.

The nineteenth-century mission service tended to be a regular feature of some Evangelical parishes, and in the twentieth century it was this wing of the Church of England which led the way. Until the full impact of the Liturgical Movement in the 1960s, Morning Prayer was the normal morning worship in Evangelical parishes. Sometimes the psalmody would be abbreviated, but sometimes it would be omitted, and hymns substituted. Canticles were reduced in number, or replaced; and the presentation of the service would be deliberately relaxed and 'folksy'. More audacious parishes shortened the confession, or omitted the creed. The sermon would be a teaching sermon, often child-orientated. One prominent exponent of this type of service was Michael Botting, who as Vicar of St Matthew's, Fulham, from 1961, soon became aware of the need for a family service in his semi-industrial parish; his experience and ideas for planning such services were outlined in *Reaching the Families* (1969) and *Teaching the Families* (1973). He was also chairman of the committee of the Church Pastoral Aid Society (CPAS) which produced the *Family Service* in 1968 (revised 1976). This was a simplified Morning Prayer, with provision for hymns and choruses in place of canticles and psalms. The sermon is called 'The Talk', and an interrogative simplified creed may replace the Apostles' Creed. This service was later incorporated into the larger *Family Worship* (1971), which included popular hymns and choruses so that the whole service was in one booklet.

This development is difficult to separate from the special services which were used for Sunday Schools and Children's Church. One popular book was *Church Teaching for the Kindergarten,* published by the Church of England Sunday

School Institute, which gave a different sample order of service for every Sunday of the Church Year. In the 1940s another popular booklet was *The Children's Church,* produced by the Church Book Room Press, a simplified form of Morning Prayer. This booklet encouraged some parishes to produce their own family services based on its structure.

Other catalysts have been special services for special occasions such as Mothering Sunday and Harvest Festival, aimed at families who perhaps rarely otherwise came to church. Mission services also have probably influenced the Family Service, ranging from the pattern of Mission Service of the Mirfield Fathers, to seaside services to holiday makers, both of which included choruses, hymns, and a mission-style address.

THE WORK OF THE LITURGICAL COMMISSION, 1966-1967

Ronald Jasper, chairman of the Church of England Liturgical Commission from 1964 to 1980, wrote that from 1965 onwards pleas for the production of an official 'Family Service' distinct from Morning and Evening Prayer were constant.[17] Many clergy were using the CPAS service or were composing their own. Archbishop Ramsey referred to this in 1966, drawing attention to the fact that section 6 of the Prayer Book (Alternative and Other Services) Measure allowed such services, giving responsibility to the minister. However, there were still requests for some official forms. The Archbishops therefore asked the Liturgical Commission to prepare a report on Informal Services, which would cover Family Services and services for special occasions. This task fell to John Wilkinson, who submitted papers to the Commission (Memorandum 74, 24.ii.1966 and 74B, 21.iv.1967). Wilkinson also prepared a short book, *Family and Evangelistic Services* (CIO 1967), which although not a Commission document contained a Foreword by Ronald Jasper commending the book to the Church. It was a book about good practice, and described structures and balance of such services, and examples of responsive psalmody and readings were given. Brian Frost contributed a note on suitable music.

The report of the Commission – 'a mere five typewritten pages'[18] – was sent to the Archbishops in June 1967. It was accepted, and presented to the House of Bishops who also accepted the Report and agreed to commend it to the dioceses. Ronald Jasper completes the story:

> Unfortunately it never became widely known, possibly because it was so short and possibly because it was never the concern of either the Convocations or the Church Assembly. The little document simply got lost in the pile of papers which descended on episcopal desks; some bishops obviously just didn't bother with it. Certainly the Commission continued to be approached by many people who had heard nothing of the Report and still wanted an official Family Service.[19]

Although section 6 of the Prayer Book (Alternative and Other Services) Measure was incorporated into the new Canons (B4 and 5), and this Report existed, agitation for official Family Services continued, and the Liturgical Commission was held responsible for their non-appearance. One suspects that piles of paper on episcopal desks have had and continue to have much to answer for!

CATALYSTS OF *PATTERNS FOR WORSHIP*

During the life of the Liturgical Commission which was responsible for *Patterns for Worship* (1989) a number of things helped the course of its work.

At the very first meeting two specific items were on the agenda. First the *Faith in the City* report, which called for a new look at services for urban priority areas. The ASB was regarded as too complex to follow (cf. the anonymous author of 1876) and something more flexible, with more concrete language and use of symbolism, was needed for this culture. The report called for a provision which will be more informal and flexible in its use of urban language, vocabulary, style and content. It will therefore reflect a universality of form with local variations, allowing significant space for worship which is genuinely local, expressed in and through local culture, and reflecting the local context.[20]

It later stated:

There has also been a clear plea that the formal liturgies so beloved of the wider Church must be complemented in the UPAs by more informal and spontaneous acts of worship and witness.[21]

Second, some bishops (notably Bishop Nigel McCulloch in the Bath and Wells Diocesan Newsletter) were airing worries about Family Services in that they were taking the place of the authorised Anglican services. (A notable example was St Peter's, Harold Wood, in the Chelmsford diocese, which had in the 1970s abandoned the cassock and surplice and had two non-Anglican Family Services each Sunday; vestments and Anglican forms only appeared when the bishop visited.) Although there was recognition that such services were popular, and often well planned, there was concern that some of them were banal, sometimes a lay person was the preacher, they were often child-orientated, and, in replacing the authorised forms, raised the question of what was Anglican worship and what was Common Prayer. Two useful publications appeared. One in 1985 was a report by the diocese of Chelmsford entitled *For the Family*. In 1982 the then bishop, John Trillo, had set up a working party to report on Family Services. Of the churches which replied to a questionnaire, 73 per cent had a Family Service. The report stated:

There now appears to be a firmly established 'family Service' tradition in Anglicanism; it persists, even though we have passed through a major period of liturgical reform; it persists outside the strict limits of authorised forms of worship, though often Family Services draw heavily upon authorised texts, or echo them, in some way.[22]

The report also listed certain characteristics of these services: non-eucharistic language which was domestic or relaxed; music which is 'church popular'; and a style of worship to incorporate both adults and children. However, the report also pointed out causes for concern: a tension between the Church family and the nuclear family; an imbalance of worship – often too didactic; banal language; and confessions which were not really confessions, and absolutions which were not real absolutions, and home-spun creeds which verged on heresy.

The second publication was the 1986 CPAS *Church Family Worship* (1988 slightly enlarged music edition) published by Hodder and Stoughton. This represents a vast expansion of *Family Worship,* aimed at both Anglican and non-Anglican congregations. It reproduces some of the ASB rites, and then offers a collection of 801 hymns, choruses, and hymn-psalms suitable for different occasions in the Church Year. This contains, as well as the ASB canticles, 785 different prayer elements – praise, thanksgiving, inter-cession, creeds etc., which can be selected to form a Family Service, including a 'Family Communion Prayer' which, although not authorised for use in the Church of England, no doubt has been and is used on some occasions in Anglican worship. CPAS reflects the trend away from a single book to a menu of liturgical fragments from a resource book, made easier also by computer text retrieval systems which allow a church to piece together and print its own special service. This book contained some very good and very varied resource material, and its sales pointed to the need for such a publication. However, certain prayers and credal pieces seemed to the Liturgical Commission to lack theological depth, and the Commission thought it would be possible to produce some consistently better material.

In 1988 the report *Children in the Way* was published, examining the place of children in the Church. The section on worship noted both the successes and weaknesses of 'Family Services':

> The attempt to involve children in worship and learning with their families – parent or parents, and other adult members of the congregation – has obviously paid dividends in some situations. If this activity of worship is as important as we think it is, many parents do want to share in it with their children. Moreover, they frequently find the teaching aimed at their children more comprehensible than the normal sermon. 'Family Services' have been sufficiently flexible to accommodate those who come without any member of their family, and can meet the needs of a wide age range.[23]

The result has been the compilation of *Patterns for Worship*. This collection attempted to rein in some of the excesses found in Family Services; provide examples of good practice; and present material which the Commission regarded as not contrary to the scriptures and the doctrine of the Church of England. It would appear that with the exception of the eucharistic material, and provided that the material does not replace authorised services, the material in *Patterns for Worship* is already legal, covered by the 1872 Act and the 1892 ruling of Convocation as well as the present Canons.

There seems little doubt concerning the popularity and, in terms of numbers, success of Family Services. The *Cambridge Evening News*, 21 May 1992, under a headline 'New-style services see churches boom', announced:

> Church congregations are booming – because ministers have adapted to new-style services, say Mid-Anglian clergymen.
> The increase has led one vicar to re-arrange his services to make them more accessible to worshippers – and put in closed-circuit television.
> A constant rise in numbers joining St Andrew's Church in Histon in the last year has meant that the Rev. Hugh McCurdy has had to take action.
> He said: 'As well as the traditional styles of worship, we have also introduced more up-to-date services, such as our weekly family service.'

And in Ely, the Rev. Alan Bartle said:

> Attendance at our informal evening service at St Mary's
> Church, Ely, has more than doubled in the past year.
> There is no set format like traditional church services and that
> is why it attracts so many people of many different ages.

A number of questions are raised by all this. Are these
services monthly 'mission' services, or the regular weekly
diet of worship for the regular congregation? Where they
seem to be the latter, then what are the ecclesiological,
liturgical and canonical relations of these services to the
statutory services? Is the Church of England now mainly a
missionary Church, needing Family Services in place of the
statutory forms which reflect a different era of Christian
commitment in the nation? But undoubtedly the most
important question facing the Church of England is
whether or not to make such forms legal *alternatives* to the
other statutory services (for it is clear that in many parishes
such services *are alternative* and *not additional to* the statutory
forms) and, if so, whether there should be some common
statutory core in order to retain some semblance of a Church
with 'Common Prayer'.

BRYAN SPINKS

NOTES

[1] See R. C. D. Jasper, *Prayer Book Revision in England 1800-1900* (SPCK:
London 1954), pp. 115ff.

[2] W. K. Clay (ed.), *Private Prayers put forth by authority during the Reign of
Queen Elizabeth* (Parker Society: Cambridge 1851).

[3] Bryan D. Spinks, *From the Lord, and 'The Best Reformed Churches'* (CLV:
Rome 1984), pp. 94-6; Patrick Collinson, *The Elizabethan Puritan Movement* (Jonathan Cape: London 1967), *passim*.

[4] John Spurr, *The Restoration Church of England 1646-1689* (Yale University Press: New Haven and London 1991), p. 187. Cf. F. C. Mather,
'Georgian Churchmanship Reconsidered: Some variations in Anglican
Public Worship 1714-1830', in *Journal of Ecclesiastical History*, 36 (1985),
pp. 255-83, esp. p. 278.

[5] Michael C. Sansom, 'Liturgical Responses to (Natural) Disaster in Seventeenth Century England', *Studia Liturgica,* 19 (1989), pp. 179-96.

[6] R. C. D. Jasper, 'The Prayer Book in the Victorian Era', in Anthony Symondson (ed.), *The Victorian Crisis of Faith* (SPCK: London 1970), pp. 107-21, p. 115.

[7] Ibid., drawing on E. Hodder, *The Life and Work of the Seventh Earl of Shaftesbury* (1886), vol. 3.

[8] W. N. Yates, *Buildings. Faith and Worship* (Clarendon Press: Oxford 1991), pp. 135-6. (Yates quotes from his earlier study *The Anglican Revival in Victorian Portsmouth* (Portsmouth 1983), pp. 5-6).

[9] Robert Braithwaite (ed.), *The Life and Letters of Rev William Pennefather, B.A.* (John F. Shaw & Co: London 1878), p. 346.

[10] London 1869, p. 4.

[11] Ibid., p. 5.

[12] Jasper, 'The Prayer Book in the Victorian Era', op. cit., p. 117, referring to Neale and Littledale.

[13] John Kent, *Holding the Fort* (Epworth Press: London 1978), p. 260. I am grateful to Canon Dr Geoffrey Rowell for his help in locating the material on Anglo-Catholic missionary services.

[14] 'Liturgical Revision', *Church Quarterly Review,* 3 (1876-7), pp. 34-63, p. 39.

[15] C. M. Davies, *Orthodox London,* Second Series (London 1875), p. 303.

[16] D. Voll, *Catholic Evangelicalism* (Faith Press: London 1963), pp. 104-5.

[17] R. C. D. Jasper, *The Development of the Anglican Liturgy 1662-1980* (SPCK: London 1989), p. 274.

[18] Ibid., p. 275.

[19] Ibid., pp. 275-6.

[20] *Faith in the City* (Church House Publishing: London 1985), para. 6.102.

[21] Ibid., para. 6.111.

[22] *For the Family,* Report of the Bishop's Working Party on Non-Statutory Worship in the Diocese of Chelmsford (Diocese of Chelmsford: Chelmsford 1986), p. 3.

[23] *Children in the Way* (NS/CHP: London 1988), para. 4.28.

8

Identity and Tradition:
A Theological Reflection

EVOLVING IDENTITY

'Identity' and 'core' both look like descriptive words, but can have an implicit prescriptive sense. 'The identity of Anglican worship' can mean what by observation are and have been its essential characteristics; we can look to see what is in the common core, the glue that has held Anglicans of various kinds together. But by 'identity' we might mean not only what Anglican worship historically has been over the centuries, but also what it ought to be now if it is to be true to its historical character. Once we move into the imperative mood, however, it is not enough to look simply to the past and the present: the identity, in the normative sense, of any Christian body and its worship must be defined also by its purpose and goal. As John Robinson once put it, according to the New Testament your doctrine of the ministry can be as high as may be, as long as your doctrine of the Church is higher, and your doctrine of the Church can be as high as may be, as long as your doctrine of the Kingdom is higher.[1]

The common core of Anglican worship in the descriptive sense has in fact never been static: from the time of Cranmer on there has been organic development, a constantly evolving identity. This has often met with resistance; there is a deep sense going back to Plato that change must be for the worse. But we must not allow the descriptive to become tacitly prescriptive, granted that any development needs critical reflection and guidance, in loyalty to the Church's historical tradition, as well as in the light of the Church's function, what it is *for*. ('New occasions teach new duties; time makes ancient good uncouth; they must upward still and onward who would keep abreast of truth').[2] Christianity is a historical religion in that it believes God has made himself known not just in history but in a particular history which he is guiding towards a goal: the redemption and salvation of the whole world.

Today there is, on the one hand, an impatience with inherited tradition, as resistant to new working of God's Spirit and to the call of mission, and on the other hand an anguished sense that sacred tradition is being abandoned, the common core of Anglican worship fragmented and its identity dissolved. Even if the uniformity of Anglican practice under the Book of Common Prayer has been exaggerated and there has been less 'common prayer' than is sometimes assumed, it is true that recent developments have done much to erode what common core there was.[3] There has been new freedom at the local level to determine the style and content of worship, encouraged by the Alternative Service Book and by the publication of *Patterns for Worship* (even though this aimed to bring home-made 'family services' under control, and secure a recognisably Anglican identity in them). One might mention more specifically the proliferation of new translations of the Bible, so that there is no common version of psalms, canticles or even the Lord's Prayer; also the alternation between 'thou' and 'you' and current moves to achieve 'inclusive language':[4] slight alterations to deeply remembered texts can be more disturbing than wholesale rewriting.

With regard to inclusive language there may be a case for playing King Canute, at least as concerns classical texts (but in the composition of new texts it is surely right to be sensitive to this issue). But if the horse has bolted, better to make the stable more accommodating than to shut the door: that is, in a situation like that of the Book of Judges, where more and more people are doing what is right in their own eyes, we should not wish simply to let the descriptive (what has been the case) be prescriptive but rather look at the rationale of prescription and work out what in our present situation needs to be prescribed. In a society which is more educated (or at any rate informed), more democratic and more culturally and religiously diverse than ever before it is important to make clear just why in worship legality and uniformity matter. In earlier times they had social and political as well as spiritual functions, to enforce loyalty to the State, when its security was under threat, and to reinforce established authority and social order.[5] Today in a more plural and mobile society, with different threats to its well-being, there will be different considerations. For example:

(1) There should be enough common core in worship for any Anglican to have a sense of belonging in any Anglican church, not just for the spiritual comfort of the individual, but so that each congregation may be sufficiently at one with itself and the wider Church to be an effective instrument of God's rule.

(2) Legality is important as relieving local leaders of having to make decisions on their own, perhaps under pressure from below, about the character of their worship, and equally as preventing them from imposing on those below their personal convictions or preferences. The legal framework gives teeth to the claim to be the Church of England, by law established.

(3) But these teeth are no longer sharp: the Church can only hope to impose what commands general assent, and the effect will be largely indirect − just as regulations in a college, though seldom read or enforced, still help to set the tone and shape the pattern of life: when the gates closed at midnight rather than staying open all night, students generally went to bed early enough to be *compos mentis* for a 9 a.m. lecture.

NEW CREATION

If regulation of worship is to command assent it must be seen to have a constructive function, and in a Church which claims to be both catholic and reformed it is important to check its function against scripture.

At first sight the New Testament has little place for inherited forms and traditions. The emphasis is on newness: new creation, new covenant, new wine needing new bottles or it will burst the old.[6] There is a new temple: Jesus was seen to have prophesied the replacement of the existing fruitless temple by a spiritual temple, the community centred on himself.[7] This temple-community saw itself as the anticipation, the outpost on earth, of the heavenly temple which would be revealed at the end of the world.[8] In other words the nature of the Church in the New Testament is eschatological: it is future-orientated, bringing the end into the present, looking towards God's final sovereignty ('Thy kingdom come') and instrumental in bringing it about. But because in Jewish thought the End will recapitulate the Beginning (*Endzeit wird Urzeit*), it is also past-orientated, in conscious continuity with God's plan and covenants from Creation onwards; it sees itself as fulfilling God's promise to Abraham, that in his posterity all the nations of the earth should be blessed. The newness of the new covenant does not abrogate the old but fulfils it (Matt. 5. 17ff); the newness of the new creation does not mean God has written off what has gone before.

We must therefore read the language of newness and discontinuity with a weather-eye to the situation addressed. Galatians, for example, gives the impression that in the new order there is no place for holy days or ritual prescriptions: the only prescriptions, the only limits on freedom, are ethical (Gal. 4. 8-10; 5. 1-6; 6. 15). But Paul is there dealing with Judaising Christians, who want to make the descriptive, the traditional ordering of the life and worship of God's people prescriptive for Gentile Christians. The

reputed 'pillars' of the new temple are by implication
building up again what they had pulled down (Gal. 2. 9, 18)
– words which recall the charge against Jesus at his trial, that
he would pull down this temple of human making and
build one without human handiwork in its place. In Paul's
view the flesh is being imposed on the spirit (Gal. 3. 3).
Between the old and the new is a sharp either/or.

RESPECT FOR TRADITION

But in Romans there are people in view who 'judge all days
to be alike', and despise those who value ritual prescriptions
(Rom. 14): there seems to be a tendency to write off the
old Jewish pattern of life and worship, perhaps as a result of
Paul's own one-sided rhetoric against Judaisers. Now Paul's
thrust is not either/or but both/and: he asserts the continuing value of Israel and the Law, and even circumcision (15.
8; 7. 12, 14; 3. 1, 2). But the old is still firmly subordinate
to the new, Sinai subordinate to Calvary, in a relationship of
fulfilment.

Paul had not yet been to Rome and perhaps had little
precise knowledge of what was going on there. But he was
writing from Corinth, which he knew only too well, and
the contempt for traditional prescriptions which he casti-
gates in Romans 14 was a feature of the Corinthian church.
1 Corinthians reveals an assumption that the kingdom has
already come (4. 8), with an over-confidence in the Spirit
and contempt of the body which leads to carelessness in
worship and life. Paul stresses the church as the body of
Christ and the temple of the Spirit, and the key word is
'build'. We have not yet arrived: the foundation has been
laid, but the building is not yet complete (3. 9ff). Both for
the individual and the church the criterion for worship and
behaviour in general is what 'builds up'. Both body and
temple must be seemly; everything must be done 'decently
and in order' (1 Cor. 14). This of course in context refers to
behaviour in church, not to a fixed order of service, but
Paul's concern for the traditions and practice of all the

churches (1 Cor. 11. 2, 16, 23) suggests the importance of a common core of liturgy and preaching for the building up of the wider church.

THE FUNCTION OF WORSHIP

This concern for order in worship is not just for the good of the church; it is because worship is what the church is *for*. Idolatry, false worship, is in the biblical view the root of all immorality. Sin from one angle may be defined as withholding worship, failing to glorify God and give him thanks (Rom. 1. 21; 3. 23), which leads to spiritual and moral blindness. In Jewish eyes, ordered worship, with a prescribed calendar, sacrifices, readings, psalms and prayers, reflects the order of heaven amid the disorder of a disaffected world; infringements of this order are attacks on heaven itself. The Judaisers in Galatia perhaps had a point. We may not believe that a home-made service or any other departure from the legally authorised forms of worship is an actual assault on heaven:[9] it may seem to be building up the local congregation. But at the same time it may in a minute way be sapping the unity of the wider Church and its power to bring the order of heaven into a world which has lost the habit of worship.

In a world so blinded and alienated from God the church must take up a stance of principled non-conformity: 'Do not be conformed to this world, but be transformed by the renewing of your minds, so that you may discern what is the will of God' (Rom. 12. 2). But such non-conformity does not necessarily entail sitting light to secular authority and order: one function of worship is to orientate God's people amid the seductions and disorder of the world, and to purify their vision so that they may see to render to God what is his, and to Caesar what God has assigned to him – also to see when Caesar transgresses his commission and becomes the seven-headed beast of Revelation. Arguably it is Romans 13 ('Let every person be subject to the governing authorities …') rather than Revelation 13 which is the odd one out in the Bible, but again the situation determines the rhetoric, and in this respect the Church of England is different from other provinces of the Anglican Communion in that it has the inherited task, and opportunity, of working with the state as part of the established order. This requires the watchful eye of a biblical prophet on human authority, secular and religious, while bearing up the pillars of it. Full-blown non-conformity is not our vocation – at the moment.

Further, in a world alienated from God, worship is not just giving God his due and keeping oneself unspotted from the world: in New Testament understanding it is a key factor in the spiritual warfare bringing creation under God's rule. It is the function of the Church to 'make known the manifold wisdom of God to the rulers and authorities in heavenly places' (Eph. 3. 10) – the spiritual powers behind human idolatry and wickedness. Ignatius told the Ephesians to 'meet more often to give thanks and glory to God. When you meet frequently, the powers of Satan are confounded, and in the face of your corporate faith his maleficence crumbles' (*Eph.* 13). For such warfare order and discipline are essential, 'for God is a God not of disorder but of peace' (1 Cor. 14. 33), and Satan represents confusion. This is not an argument for prescribed forms or a common core, but rather (whether we share the mythological attitudes of the first century or not) for recovering the sense that what we do in church and how we do it matters eternally, because worship is instrumental in bringing God's kingdom, and because we are joining with all the company of heaven.

For the Church is an outpost, a colony of heaven on earth; like the colonies of Athens or Aegina it is to bring the life and values of the mother city here and now into barbarian places, until God's kingdom comes on earth as in heaven. So in its worship it must hold together both 'now' and 'not yet', God intimately present and God infinitely beyond. The BCP style is strong on 'not yet' and 'beyond' ('bring us to everlasting life', celebrant facing east, God as sovereign and judge), while the ASB style perhaps over-reacts ('keep us in life eternal', celebrant facing the people, with Abba Father familiarly present).[10] It is no answer to go back to what used to be the case; rather, move forward to an ethos which combines both, as does the New Testament, taken as a whole.

RESIDENT ALIENS

In such a perspective how much 'common core' is needed? On the one hand, form and content need to be provisional and adaptable. In the New Testament there are what look like liturgical formulas and nascent creeds, but they are few and brief, and there is no uniformity of text, not even in the Lord's Prayer or the eucharistic words. Prophets were free to improvise. Christians took over the Jewish method of 'contemporising' scripture; shifts of application brought with them modifications of the text itself. They were not bound by the past; the Spirit was their guide. As 'aliens and exiles' (1 Peter 1. 1; 2. 11) Christians must travel light: 'Jesus said, "The world is a bridge; pass over it. Do not build houses on it"'.[11] The larger and more uniform the common core, the greater the resistance to necessary change and new movements of the Spirit.

On the other hand, the *paroikoi* of 1 Peter are *resident aliens;* Christians need to be sufficiently at home to be able to function constructively. There must be a strong element of the fixed and familiar: travelling light still requires a 'knapsack', such as Alan Wilkinson pleaded for in the *Church Times* (1 May 1992), a common core for corporate and personal use. This is not the place to specify what it might comprise, but if any future prescription to this end is to win the assent of those who look to the leading of the Holy Spirit, and mission rather than maintenance, and is to overcome the upset caused by unfamiliar forms of worship and differences of wording, then what is prescribed must be clearly seen to be serving the Church's purpose and goal.

There must be education with regard to what we are doing in worship and why.

We have strongly asserted the claims of the future (the Church's task and goal), and the newness of the new covenant in which God's Spirit gives a freedom from the past and ability to improvise. We have noted also the claims of the past, and in conclusion may point to the fundamental importance of the Christian story ('salvation history') in shaping not just Anglican identity but ecumenical Christian identity, apart from which Anglicanism would be a trivial pursuit. It has been said that there is no hope of peace in Northern Ireland until Catholic and Protestant children sit down and learn history together. A deeply shared past, a deeply shared family history, gives a more profound unity and identity than surface uniformity in worship. Since Christians learn and assimilate their past from the Bible, for the most part through its public reading and exposition, the framing of a common lectionary – ecumenically common – is a crucial area for prescription, bringing out the continuity as well as discontinuity between Old Covenant and New. In striving to maintain our Anglican identity and common prayer we must, Janus-like, look both forward and backward; and we must not try to do it on our own.

JOHN SWEET

NOTES

[1] See K. M. Carey (ed.), *The Historic Episcopate* (Dacre Press: London 1954), p. 17.

[2] J. Russell Lowell, *English Hymnal* 563.

[3] See Chapter 9, pp. 82-6ff.

[4] See *Making Women Visible* (Church House Publishing: London 1989).

[5] See Chapter 3, pp. 21.

[6] In Luke's version Jesus recognises ironically that this goes against normal preference: 'No one after drinking old wine desires new wine, for he says "The old is good."' (Luke 5. 39).

[7] Mark interweaves the story of the cleansing of the Temple with that of the withered fig tree (Mark 11. 12-23; cf. 14. 58; John 2. 19-21).

[8] This is the probable sense of the 'pillars' metaphor at Gal. 2. 9; cf. Rev. 3. 12.

[9] See Dan. 7. 25; 8. 9-13; the 'little horn', in suppressing the seasons and sacrifices of the Temple, is attacking the heavenly hosts and throwing down the stars.

[10] But ASB has many advances on BCP. See Chapter 2.

[11] An 'unwritten saying' of Jesus inscribed by Akbar on a building in his abandoned capital, Fatehpur Sikri, near Agra.

PART 2

9

Promoting a Common Core

A NEW STRATEGY

The Liturgical Commission believes that the question of
common prayer – that is, of whether there will continue to
be patterns of prayer which unite English Anglicans past and
present in their worship of God – is an important question
that needs to be addressed at national, diocesan and parish
level.

Discussion about common prayer is often confused; the
first part of this book has tried to throw some light on the
issues raised in such debate. The purpose of this chapter is to
sketch the outlines of a strategy that the Liturgical Commission believes the Church of England could follow in the
future. The concept which it suggests should lie at the heart
of this strategy is that of a common core to the Church's
worship. This is not to imply a completely static centre to
the praying life of the Church of England. As Kenneth
Stevenson has helpfully noted, such a core is always in the
process of change, shedding old elements and gathering new
ones. The liturgical core cannot simply be the creation of
official bodies in the Church. However the Commission
would urge that the future health of the Church of England
requires that attention be given to identifying, cherishing
and promoting an evolving core to the Church's worship.

It is the presence of considerable creativity and vitality at
many points in the worshipping life of the Church of
England that makes this question important. Official and
unofficial changes in worship in the Church of England,
often good in themselves, have the potential to undermine
the unity of the Church and confuse the devotional life of

its members. Is it inevitable that creativity at congregational level will mean that English Anglicans can no longer feel at home in different parish churches? Must the sensitive adaptation of worship to local culture[1] lead to the formation of personal patterns of devotion that are more parochial than national or catholic? Are liturgical anarchy and the fragmentation of personal spirituality an inevitable result of increasing deregulation of public worship? The answer, in the mind of the Commission, is to give attention to the evolving core of the Church's common prayer.

THE STARTING POINT

The first part of this book has endeavoured to explore some of the factors that have shaped the idea of common prayer in the Church of England. Clearly, it is a mistake to imagine that there was one static form of common prayer before 1965, when the process of authorising new services began. Some elements of worship, in particular liturgical texts and clerical vesture, were governed by law. Others, such as hymns or music, were not subject to significant legal control. Common prayer, in the sense of a pattern of prayer which bound many English Anglicans together, was largely woven out of required texts and deregulated hymnody. In many ways the great tradition of English hymnody arose precisely because the central texts of the liturgy were fixed and effectively out of the control of the Church.

As has been shown, the common prayer that largely prevailed in the Church of England before 1965 was not without its critics. The chaplains in the First World War noted and analysed the almost total alienation of the common man from the Church's liturgy.[2] Extensive use was made at parochial level of forms of worship other than those provided in the Book of Common Prayer.[3] Bishop Frere, a major liturgical scholar in the early years of the century, attributed ignorance amongst Anglicans about the character and form of Christian worship to its rigid control by law. He predicted that liturgical reform in England would require 'a long period of authorised experiment' before the Church would be in a position to form 'instructed judgements'.[4]

Perhaps the most significant factor fracturing any experience of common prayer in the Church of England has been the sharp polarisation between the Protestant and Catholic wings of the Church. At many levels the interaction between these two great traditions has been extremely fruitful, not least in recovering a doctrine of the Church and in a deepening appreciation of the eucharist.[5] However, at the level of parish worship the results often undermined a genuine sense of common life. The significance of much liturgical practice lay primarily in what it denied or whom it excluded. Although both traditions laid claim to the Book of Common Prayer, people's experience of 'common prayer' was intimately bound up with party allegiance and even with rejection of their bishop. A major casualty has often been the sense of liturgical common life within a diocese.

One of the achievements of the ASB has been progress towards a recognisable and unitive pattern for parochial eucharistic worship on a Sunday morning. In the framing of the new services, careful and painstaking discussion, sometimes resulting in responsible reserve on controversial matters, led to a surprising degree of convergence over texts, structure and theology. The parochial style that has arisen around Rite A in many parishes owes a great deal both to the Parish Communion movement and to the charismatic movement. It has been welcomed in a Church wearied by a century and a half of controversy over the eucharist. It may even be that its very success in uniting the Church of England has deprived almost a generation of worshippers and clergy of a sense of this achievement.

At the same time the emergence of the 'ordinary' Rite A eucharist as part of the common core has taken place at the expense of a major earlier element of the core, namely the familiar words of the Book of Common Prayer and of

Sunday worship that centred on Morning and Evening Prayer. The Episcopal Church in the United States of America may have chosen a better way in printing new and old language services together in one *Book of Common Prayer* (1979). There have been recent signs of some *rapprochement* with those bereaved by the loss of the old liturgy.[6] This has been helped by widespread dissatisfaction with the terse, even bare, liturgical language of the 1960s and 1970s and a desire to find a richer and more evocative liturgical language.[7] In preparing the two resource books *Patterns for Worship* and *The Promise of His Glory* the Liturgical Commission was conscious of being caught between the need for vivid, accessible, contemporary language and the yearning for potent historic resonance.

While many members of the Church of England may feel content with the degree of convergence established by the ASB there are many signs that the position is not stable. Developments that may erode or change the common core include:

(1) Many parishes are moving on from the Parish Communion style. The concerns that give rise to this vary. Some feel the pressure of squeezing the whole of a congregation's liturgical life into one hour on a Sunday morning. Some are attracted by new styles of worship or feel confident enough to explore less well known options permitted in Rite A. Some are responding to a desire for non-eucharistic services.

(2) Many parishes are developing a variety of 'local' practices. These may be adopted for cultural or mission reasons and may find their inspiration in contemporary Christian movements. This tendency has been fostered in part by the more permissive attitude the ASB takes to determining elements of worship at the parish level.

(3) A variety of influential reports have criticised the pastoral adequacy of official liturgical provision in the Church of England.[8] There has been increasing recognition of the drawing power of 'Family Services' and the recognition that

these must be seen as 'another strand' within Church of England worship.[9] These criticisms led to the Liturgical Commission's report *Patterns for Worship*. A revised version of the educational and liturgical material that does not require synodical authorisation is due to be published. An alternative, more flexible form of Morning and Evening Prayer is being discussed by Synod. Alternative eucharistic prayers that attempt to take seriously the criticisms that the prayers of the ASB are bland and conceptual are under discussion.

(4) *Lent, Holy Week, Easter* and *The Promise of His Glory* have made available wider seasonal provision. These may be supplemented by unofficial provision along similar lines.[10] (Seasonal material, of course, was almost completely suppressed by Cranmer in the interests of simplicity and uniformity. There is plenty of evidence that modern sensibility differs from him over this.)

(5) Shifts in the way language about men and women is heard and used has led to new policies on the part of publishers and educationalists. Some impact on liturgical language is inevitable. The Liturgical Commission's own discussion of the issue is to be found in *Making Women Visible* (1989).

(6) Printing played an important part in fixing liturgical texts. The availability of relatively cheap word-processing and photocopying will increase the creation of liturgies at parish level that draw on a variety of sources, official and unofficial.

(7) In the years following the publication of the Second Vatican Council's Constitution on the Sacred Liturgy in 1963, ecumenical developments have contributed to the strengthening of the common core. With the publication of the revised agreed common texts *Praying Together*[11] this convergence will continue for major texts. However, recent years have seen a burst of creative liturgical writing in virtually all the major liturgical traditions. Many denominations

have new service books in preparation. While these often draw on common understanding, it is possible that the common core between the Christian traditions may be put under stress in the short term.

THE IDEA OF A COMMON CORE

Behind the idea of a common core for the Church of England lie a number of principles that merit some exploration.

1. Liturgy provides a recognisable structure for church life

Common patterns affirm common life. They enable Christians from different congregations to recognise each other as part of one Church. They enable people to tune in to the life and worship of a different congregation from their own.

The common patterns in the liturgical life of the Church originate at different levels. Some are simply part of the given of God's revelation: Baptism, Sunday assembly, public reading of Scripture, and Eucharist. Some are venerable and appropriate structures that respond to these divine givens; an example is the traditional shape of the Sunday Assembly; Word—Prayer—Eucharist. Others reflect the created potentiality of human beings, such as singing and music, or arise from the ordinary dynamic of human communities, such as the need for agreed arrangements, common memory and language. Some may be quite particular to a given culture, such as traditions of welcome or dress.

Common patterns of worship are an important part of how the character and identity of the Christian Church are made visible within the wider human community. At the level of witness these patterns can point to the Church's faith in Jesus Christ and to the character of the new humanity that God is creating. Such visible expressions of the Church's faith are open to the ambiguity inherent in much symbolism; the same pattern may speak to one person of the abiding character of the Gospel and to another of the alienating pretensions of a social elite. Discernment is no easy matter. Nor can the evolution of patterns of worship simply be manipulated by experts; popular response and intuition play an important part in the establishment of patterns of common prayer.[12]

Jurgen Moltmann has noted the capacity of ritual (i.e. developed Christian forms) to exclude and repel those outside the worshipping life of the Church.[13] Some churches attempt to avoid this danger by abandoning all distinctive Christian practices in the name of effective evangelism. This means that believers are not helped to find appropriate expressions of their life of faith. A better way accepts the need for distinct patterns of worship, guards against a closed and excluding spirit, and then provides ways of welcoming newcomers and inducting them into the worshipping patterns of the Church.

In exploring the concept of a common core to Church of England worship it may be helpful to note a number of ways in which such common patterns operate:

(1) People do not need to be equally familiar with every part of the common core. The whole of the core does not need to be used invariably; for many persons recognition is sufficient. Diversity also has a part to play in building up a sense of common identity.

(2) A number of different factors will affect how quickly the core can change without damage. Within church life new patterns can establish themselves rapidly where they meet a pastoral need or correspond to a theological or cultural intuition. Large gatherings and the media play a significant part in the spread of new elements. Weekly, annual and life rhythms all have to be taken into account in assessing the rate of change that is beneficial.

(3) Public liturgy is part of the interface of world and Church. Here stability can be a benefit where the core is itself pastorally helpful. The acceptable rate of change from

this perspective is particularly dependent on cultural changes, on the media and on educational patterns.

Amongst the most problematic changes have been those that disturb resonances within the culture's literary canon. Very important is the translation of the Bible that is read or drawn on in liturgical composition. Translations such as the RSV, NIV, NRSV, which echo the phrasing and principles of the Authorised Version, can minimise difficulty here. A strong case can certainly be made that the Church of England should adopt one version of the Bible for public use. The most likely candidate would be the NRSV, which appears to be gaining ground in many circles. Such a policy would, however, face strong resistance from parishes and individuals committed to other versions. The NRSV's sensitivity to inclusive language for human beings will commend it to some and provoke the suspicions of others.

Very often it is changes in society rather than the Church which create the difficulty: the literary canon itself changes; the Bible is no longer taught in schools; a different style of English is given educational priority. (It is just possible that current shifts in educational policy may reverse these tendencies somewhat.) Equally a living Church, giving voice to authentic Christian faith, will be creating new cultural resonance.

Perceptions of how liturgy effects English society will vary. Historically the Christian Church has acted as a midwife to important areas of English culture and many will see modern developments as a sort of divorce in which both parties are partly to blame. Others will take a less pessimistic view of changes in Church or society. The Christian faith has shown a striking ability to adapt to different cultures and to give rise to liturgical forms which both affirm and criticise the society in which the Gospel is taking root. Like Abraham, the church looks forward to a city that is to come 'whose builder and maker is God' (Heb. 11. 10, 14-16, 13.13).

2. Liturgy provides a framework for the individual Christian

Familiar patterns and texts play an important part in structuring and deepening the discipleship of individual Christians. People's capacity for constructive change in this area will depend on temperament, on personal and spiritual growth, on the ordinary human life-cycle, and on the ways in which they are affected by cultural changes in society and Church.

Recent emphasis on forming a corporate spirituality based on the parish eucharist has risked neglecting the need individuals have for usable devotional resources. Canon Alan Wilkinson's article in the *Church Times* calling for an Anglican knapsack on which individuals could draw in a crisis has already been referred to.[14] He suggested that what was needed was a knapsack,

> small and compact enough for emergencies, profound enough to express a lifetime's sorrows and joys, a common core for corporate and personal use. So it should include (for example) a simple daily office (with lessons of only a few verses), a selection of psalms, hymns, collects, litanies, canticles; an outline form of the eucharist; forms for anointing, confession, sick communion, commendation of the dying and the dead; a form of the rosary acceptable to Anglicans; some of the mantras made familiar by Taizé . . . ; and parts of the (undervalued) Revised Catechism of 1962. There is no reason why some of the material should not be in Prayer Book language . . .

While the detail of this proposal obviously needs discussion – not least an apparent implication that the Bible is a bit beyond lay people – the idea is important and builds on the interaction that needs to exist between corporate worship and personal prayer. The 1985-90 Liturgical Commission suggested that the ASB might be replaced by a Sunday Book, a book for Daily Prayer, a book of Pastoral

Offices, and a seasonal resource book.[15] Others may prefer
the policy of the Book of Common Prayer and of other
Anglican provinces in trying to combine a Sunday Service
Book and a personal primer. (Some fear that the multiplica-
tion of books may undermine common prayer; in reality the
alternative to official books is not less diversity but simply
more private enterprise.)

Individual Christians need to build up a spiritually
constructive understanding of the Church's liturgical forms.
In the past this depended mainly on unofficial pastoral
processes within different traditions in the Church. In much
contemporary evangelism there is no mechanism or context
in which such liturgical formation of the individual can take
place. The result can be a profound alienation. The absence
of appropriate methods of such liturgical formation can lead
sensitive ministers to abandon patterns of worship that
would be profoundly enriching if their inner genius could
be communicated. Often liturgical formation is limited to
theological colleges, encouraging the notion that liturgy is a
clerical preserve. One of the great strengths of catechumenal
approaches to evangelism is that they can enable people to
relate helpfully to valuable liturgical forms.

IDENTIFYING THE CORE

1. Patterns and Structures

An important element in the common core is service shape
and structure with the flow and movement to which such
structure naturally gives rise. Traditional Anglicans coped
with a wide variety of hymns because they were at home
with the shape of the service. It has been an important
insight of modern liturgical study that it is shape rather than
particular texts that provide the common core, the 'deep
structure', of the major acts of Christian worship.[16] Important examples include:

For the eucharist:

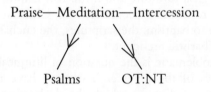

Word – Intercession – Eucharist

OT – Apostolic – Gospel
Reading

Thanksgiving—Communion—Dedication

For daily prayer:

Praise—Meditation—Intercession

Psalms   OT:NT

The flow within a unit often plays an important part in forming the Church's understanding. The different ways in which the reading of scripture is structured in the eucharist ('Christ at the centre') and the office (a conversation in which the two Testaments complement each other) have played an important part in forming the way Anglicans interpret scripture. In public prayer an order World—Church—Needy or Church—World—Needy reflects the structure of the Lord's Prayer and gives an appropriate shape to the Church's priestly work of intercession.

Robert Taft notes the way certain 'soft points' in the eucharist attract enrichment that can eventually overburden the liturgy. He mentions the preparation, the movement from reading to the eucharistic prayer, and the post-communion.[17] Kenneth Stevenson has proposed significant clarifications at the soft points in Rite A which will need to be taken into account when the ASB services are reviewed.[18] At some of these points the ASB allows quite a variety of options. Some would argue that the core would be clearer if these options were reduced; so, for example, allowing only one place for the Prayers of Penitence. Others believe that provided the main outlines of the shape are made vividly clear by catechesis and presentation, some flexibility elsewhere may enhance people's grasp of the core.

2. Presentation

The way in which liturgy is presented is obviously an important part of the common core. Particularly important are the arrangement of the liturgical space and the use of certain liturgical furniture and dress. It is helpful if the space and furniture express accurately the Christian assembly's relationship to baptism, the scriptures, the eucharistic action, and the eucharistic president.

More problematic is the question of liturgical dress. The controversies of the nineteenth century have made this a painful topic of division which the declarations of Canon B 8.5 have not altogether removed. There is a danger that this legacy still inhibits either appropriate care or the emergence of a practice that can unite English Anglicans. Recent debates in General Synod have made it clear that there is little desire to see liturgical vesture abandoned for normal public worship.

Questions of the quality and appropriate style of presentation should not be seen simply as matters of ecclesiastical politics. They profoundly affect people's experience of worship and deserve care and a sense of proportion about past controversy. Attention has to be given to 'presiding skills' and to the way in which gesture, posture and movement can make or mar a congregation's prayer.

3. Familiar words

Prayers, creeds and canticles obviously form a very important part of the common core. Some will belong to the core simply because of their place in the structure of the rites; others gain a place in the core because of the affection they inspire. At the moment texts from both the Prayer Book and the ASB are to be found in the core. It will be important that 'experts' do not intervene too abruptly in this process of discernment but that older texts be given a chance to show whether they are really established as elements of the core.

The core cannot simply be equated with the mandatory parts of a rite but will include those other elements that become important to the people of God. The mandatory parts of a rite indicate the essential structure of a rite, or points of theological difficulty or sensitivity; they may or may not be part of the core.

(i) *Congregational Texts*

The responses, dialogues and acclamations of the eucharist are obviously part of the common core. This is probably also true of certain familiar elements of the daily office.

The Roman Catholic body ICEL is currently involved in revising its translation of the Missal. In general it is proposing no change in congregational texts. However two likely changes may affect Anglican use.[19] After the first two readings at the eucharist they are proposing to change 'This is the word of the Lord' to 'The word of the Lord'. In the opening dialogue of the eucharist the proposal is to replace 'It is right to give him thanks and praise' with 'It is right to give our thanks and praise'. (The latter is equally close to the Latin 'Dignum et justum est'.)

Certain prayers are probably established as part of the core:
- the Confessions from the Book of Common Prayer and the ASB
- the Collect for Purity

- the Prayer of Humble Access
- the Post-Communion prayers of Rite A
- the General Thanksgiving
- traditional versions of the Magnificat, Nunc Dimittis, Gloria in Excelsis and the Nicene Creed
- the Evening Collects (BCP and ASB)
- many collects (e.g. Advent 1, Ash Wednesday, Easter 4, Quinquagesima = Pentecost 7)
- the prayers of St Richard of Chichester and St Ignatius Loyola (which do not owe their popularity to authorisation)
- the Burial Anthem ('In the midst of life' etc.)

Some of these owe their place in the core to familiar musical settings. Many newer liturgical compositions of quality still wait for musical settings to match.

An interesting issue arises with those canticles such as the Te Deum and the Gospel canticles whose familiarity has depended on attendance at sung Sunday offices. If these are to be preserved for the common core it may be necessary to introduce them on occasions into the Sunday eucharist. The Gospel canticles can be used between the readings. The Te Deum could occasionally replace the Gloria in Excelsis in the opening rite of the eucharist. (Those who dislike the modern Te Deum found in the ASB may look with more favour on the more poetic and familiar wording to be found in the new ecumenical collection *Praying Together*.)

A particular difficulty arises with the Lord's Prayer. There have clearly been disadvantages in changing these familiar words at the point at which Christian influence in schools has been declining. The matter has not been helped by the fact that a variety of modern translations are in use. The ecumenical Joint Liturgical Group has recently attempted to lessen the confusion by making two recommendations. First, that the 'modified traditional version' ('who art', 'those who trespass') should be used in ecumenical gatherings. Secondly that schools should be urged to use and teach either the 'modified traditional' or the modern version to be found in the ASB, or both.

(ii) *Prayer Structures*

Often what contributes to the common core is not an exact form of words but a recognisable prayer structure. The familiar shape of the collect remains a fine part of our tradition of prayer which needs to be taught and used.[20] Litanies and responses are an effective and popular form of prayer; recent liturgical books have sought to extend the range of these and to bring them to the attention of service leaders.

Clearly the eucharistic prayer stands in a category of its own. Experience suggests that many clergy and laity have yet to understand that it is to be seen as one prayer with a movement of its own: an opening proclamation (Latin *praefatio*) of praise that then resolves into memorial, invocation, petition and self-dedication. An understanding of the dynamic movement of the prayer is not helped if the narrative of institution is treated as a fixed formula of consecration, or if no variation is allowed in the form or position of prayer for the Holy Spirit. The eucharistic prayers of the ASB may appear dull and conceptual when compared with those of other provinces in the Anglican communion. The Liturgical Commission has received many representations urging that more vivid and responsive eucharistic prayers are needed if this central prayer of the eucharistic action is to hold its own in the common core.

4. Agreed norms and boundaries

The common core is eroded when elements are introduced which clash strongly with received Anglican doctrine or which raise conscientious difficulties for significant groups of Anglicans. Within the worshipping life of the Church the common core is sustained and protected by accepted norms and boundaries. It is a positive aspect of Anglican ethos that norms play a more important part than boundaries. Norms are communicated by example as well as by official endorsement in authorised texts and regulations. (Appendix 2 of *Patterns for Worship* gives some guidance on discerning doctrinal boundaries.)[21]

Increased deregulation places additional responsibility on ordained ministers and other liturgical leaders to be aware of these norms and to respect the boundaries operating in Church of England worship. If the greater discretion now being given to individual liturgical leaders is not to be destructive there needs to be a much stronger commitment to their liturgical formation.

5. Hymnody

Hymns are obviously a very important part of the common core of Church of England worship although they are not subject to ecclesiastical regulation. The hymnic part of the core is shaped by a number of influences. These include popular sentiment; structural factors such as RSCM and the publication of hymnbooks; and, the impact of certain movements within the Church, for example the Evangelical, Anglo-Catholic and Charismatic movements.

The role of movements in establishing hymnody within the common liturgical core highlights the importance of a shared Christian commitment in creating such a core. Love, respect and fellowship are inescapable elements in creating and sustaining such a core.

Other Churches – including some other Anglican provinces – may find the absence of regulation in the Church of England both odd and unhealthy. It is interesting how little discussion the Joint Liturgical Group's *Singing the Faith*[22] has provoked in Anglican circles.

This part of the core has grown up without official recognition. As a channel of popular devotion it has introduced into Anglican life the contribution of the Methodist,

Evangelical, Catholic and Charismatic revivals and thus plays an important part in forming Anglican identity. Many important elements of this hymnic core are now under threat and it could be argued that some deliberate attempts are needed to preserve it. One practical suggestion would be for a parish or deanery to identify a core list of traditional hymns that they wish to keep in use and then make a deliberate attempt to teach and enjoy them.

SUSTAINING THE COMMON CORE

In many ways an evolving common core will continue to be part of the worshipping life of any communion whether or not it is given particular attention. However, greatly increased flexibility at parochial level calls for the development of some deliberate strategy to sustain a healthy core to Church of England worship. A number of steps in this strategy can be identified.

1. Identification

Attention needs to be given to recognising the importance of maintaining a common liturgical core and to identifying its significant elements. This chapter seeks to contribute to this process and the Liturgical Commission clearly has a role in this. Identification of, and reflection on, this common core needs to take place at many levels of church life.

2. Fellowship

Clerical individualism and parochial isolationism are major barriers to the sustaining of a liturgical core. Christian leaders and parishes need to attend not only 'to their own interests but also to the interests of others' (Phil. 2. 4). Real fellowship and respect across parochial boundaries must be an important element in sustaining a common core. Also important is a positive, though not necessarily uncritical, appreciation of the different movements that arise in church life.

3. Education

More attention needs to be given to the continuing liturgical formation of ordained ministers and other liturgical leaders. This should be done in an atmosphere which encourages respect for and healthy interaction between different strands of church life. It will involve new educational priorities, leadership by the Bishops and proper resourcing of the Liturgical Commission and of national and diocesan liturgical officers and bodies.

It remains astonishing that so important an area of church life is so under-resourced. Often diocesan liturgical groups or committees are treated as peripheral to diocesan strategy and their members are regarded as eccentric and possibly dangerous enthusiasts. In many places there seems to be little awareness that worship is central to the creative renewal of the Church. One factor that contributes to the present lack of understanding or leadership is the fact that liturgy is not a major element in English theology departments. The contrast with the situation on the Continent or in North America is striking.

4. Regulation

The framework of official regulation of worship needs to be more widely known and respected. This involves encouraging a better understanding of its function – faithfulness to the Gospel and to each other – a better style of communication and a healthier grasp of the relationship between norms and boundaries. There are challenges here to the style of English ecclesiastical law and its comparative alienation from theological, pastoral and liturgical principle and scholarship. In recent years copyright procedures applying to local editions have been greatly simplified so that parishes able to work within certain broad conditions can reproduce without having to ask for permission. The official guidelines also make it clear that variations not provided for in the text or rubrics of the services may be discussed with the diocesan authorities. This policy invites a more integrated approach to the oversight of worship at a diocesan level. To put it more crudely, diocesan liturgical groups and advisers need to be fostered and respected.

Anglicans will have to rise above a literal but anti-liturgical approach to church regulation of worship. In a situation where there are few practical constraints on a minister's freedom this will require, in Alan Wilkinson's words, 'a degree of discipline and self-abnegation unfamiliar to many Anglicans'. This, in turn, is unlikely to arise unless hard-pressed churches feel that they are being offered liturgical advice and material which meet the demands of their responsibility for mission and pastoral care.

5. Publication

Printed liturgical material, both books and people's service cards, will continue to play an important part in establishing and sustaining the common core. It is therefore important that care should continue to be given to the preparation of official liturgical texts and their authorisation or commendation.

It is difficult to assess what the effect of computers will be in this area. The idea of a Prayer Book has played an important part in designating the liturgical core here and in other Anglican provinces. Discussion will continue as to whether the ASB should be replaced by a series of service books on the Roman Catholic model or by a core Prayer Book supplemented by other liturgical books as has been done by the Episcopal Church in the United States of America. In either event there would be a case for printing an outline people's service before the full text of a service. This would make the shape of the liturgy clear but would not include variable ministerial texts. These could then be printed separately for Sunday or occasional use with numbered alternative congregational texts in an appendix, somewhat in the manner of a hymnbook. There may also be a case for an official personal primer, to which individual publishers or groups could add further devotional material.

MICHAEL VASEY

NOTES

[1] 'Down to Earth Worship': the Statement of the Third International Anglican Liturgical Consultation, York 1989, in *Liturgical Inculturation in the Anglican Communion*, ed. David R. Holeton (Alcuin/GROW 1990).

[2] *The Church in the Furnace*, ed. F. C. Macnutt (1917).

[3] See Chapter 7.

[4] R. C. D. Jasper, *The Development of the Anglican Liturgy 1662-1980* (SPCK 1989), pp. 86-7.

[5] 'Eucharistic Theology' by Christopher Cocksworth in *The Identity of Anglican Worship*, ed. Kenneth Stevenson and Bryan Spinks (Mowbray 1991), pp. 49-68.

[6] See Michael Perham (ed.), *Model and Inspiration* (SPCK 1993).

[7] Cf. *Patterns for Worship*, GS 898 (Church House Publishing 1989), *The Promise of His Glory* (CHP/Mowbray 1991), *Praying Together*, English Language Liturgical Consultation (Canterbury Press 1990), and (First), *Second*, and *Third Progress Report on the Revision of the Roman Missal* (ICEL 1988, 1990, 1992).

[8] *Faith in the City* (Church House Publishing 1985); *Children in the Way* (NS/CHP 1988).

[9] *For the Family* (Diocese of Chelmsford) p. 4.

[10] Michael Perham (ed.), *Enriching the Christian Year* (SPCK 1993).

[11] For some account of the Church of England's contribution to this revision see Appendix 1 of *Making Women Visible* (Church House Publishing 1989).

[12] Mary Collins, *Contemplative Participation* (Liturgical Press, Minnesota, 1990), pp. 9-22; cf. Trevor Lloyd et al., *Introducing Patterns for Worship* (Grove Books 1990), p. 18.

[13] *Church in the Power of the Spirit* (SCM Press 1975), pp. 261-75.

[14] See Chapter 8, p. 75.

[15] *The Worship of the Church as it approaches the Third Millenium*, GS Misc 364 (CHP 1991), pp. 18ff.

[16] For an influential discussion of the significance of 'deep structure' and 'soft points' for liturgical form see Robert Taft, *Beyond East and West: Problems in Liturgical Understanding* (The Pastoral Press, Washington, 1984), pp. 151ff.

[17] Ibid., pp. 160-1.

[18] 'Soft Points in the Eucharist', in Michael Perham (ed.), *Liturgy for a New Century* (SPCK/Alcuin 1991), pp. 29-43.

[19] *Third Progress Report* on the Revision of the Roman Missal (ICEL 1992), pp. 18, 28.

[20] See Introduction to *The Collects from the Alternative Service Book 1980* (Mowbray/SPCK 1987), quoting *A Companion to the Alternative Service Book* by R. C. D. Jasper and Paul F. Bradshaw (SPCK 1986), pp. 265ff.

[21] Also in *Ecumenical Relations: Ecumenical Canons B43 and B44, Code of Practice* (General Synod 1989), p. 32.

[22] Ed. Charles Robertson (Canterbury Press 1990).

10

The Training of Clergy and Readers

LITURGICAL FORMATION

It is the clergy of the Church of England, together with others licensed to conduct Anglican worship, who have often been blamed for the loss of common prayer in the contemporary Church. Disillusionment with the Book of Common Prayer, the imposition of new services on unwilling congregations, the adoption of change for change's sake, ignorance of the spirit of the Worship and Doctrine Measure 1974 – during the last fifteen years or so, all these charges have been laid at the feet of clergy, Readers and others licensed to conduct public worship. Whatever the truth of these accusations, it is apparent that the moral influence and legal rights of the incumbent have often been perceived to be working contrary to the spirit of maintaining and developing an evolving core of Anglican common prayer. Fingers are pointed at theological colleges and courses, at training incumbents and at Readers' and post-ordination training courses; and questions are asked about the adequacy of the liturgical formation of those with responsibility for the conduct of Anglican worship. If those who conduct our worship have little clear idea about the significance and nature of common prayer, what hope is there that the wider Church will be able to share in that vision, and benefit from its fruits?

Several factors might be identified as key to the liturgical formation of those who conduct public worship. Of primary importance is the individual's experience of liturgical worship before, during and after their training. If, as the educationalists tell us, the most effective and profound modes of learning are those where the learner actively participates in the learning event, preferably on a regular basis, then regular attendance at liturgical worship can be expected to have some effect on the worshipper. That is how worship is done, this is how the person conducting the worship behaves, that is what worshippers are expected to do . . . and so on. The messages about the nature of the worship event received by the worshippers during an act of worship may not be consciously recognised, but they can be very powerful nonetheless.

Reflection upon acts of worship, and the passing on of oral traditions about worship, may also play a powerful part in the liturgical formation of the group or individual. The priest who tells a server how, when, where and why to move as she serves is *de facto* telling her something about the character of the worship, and her part in it. When she later comes to offer herself for Reader ministry, the ex-server ought to be given the opportunity to ask some profound theological questions about the nature of the eucharist and to re-evaluate the roles of the different people who participate in it.

Liturgical formation may also be greatly influenced by factors well beyond the experience of or reflection upon liturgy itself. Pastoral and theological priorities may provoke a radical re-evaluation of an individual's attitudes towards liturgical worship. A parish weekend away may highlight a real need for more opportunities for spontaneity in the regular Sunday pattern of worship. As a congregation begins to discover for itself the costliness of what it means to be part of the body of Christ, the nature and form of the intercessions and confession may need to be reviewed. A series of Lent groups on the nature of the Church might provoke the congregation and incumbent to reconsider the ways in which their local church relates to the wider Church in its worship.

These considerations are often interrelated and complex. There are always questions about the interaction of an individual's hopes and fears for worship, the hopes and fears of the wider congregation, and the demands and expectations of the wider Church. Liturgical formation does not and cannot take place in a vacuum. It is a process to which many people and events contribute.

WHY BOTHER WITH LITURGICAL FORMATION?

Liturgical formation has to do with setting the worshipper free to worship God 'in spirit and in truth', be they lay person, deacon, priest, Reader or bishop. It involves a sufficient familiarity with the givens of liturgical worship that those givens do not obscure the gospel and the worshipper's response to it. Rather, the liturgical formation of the worshipper should enable them to hear and respond to the gospel through word and sacrament regularly.

Good liturgical formation will involve the worshipper in understanding not only how liturgical worship works, and their part in it, but also why the liturgy is shaped in the way it is. A clear understanding of the shape and dynamics of the eucharist can greatly enhance a worshipper's active participation in the acts of thanksgiving and communion. In other words, good liturgical formation is one means of ensuring that the worship in which we share is edifying, building up the faith and witness of the people of God.

The liturgical formation of those who conduct worship has also one further aim at heart; that of enabling the worshipping congregation themselves to be 'formed'. Liturgical formation for clergy and Readers involves more than simple familiarity with the traditions and books used in this local church here and now. It involves an appreciation of, and some familiarity with, the forms and traditions of worship in the wider Church. It also involves the ability to recognise when to share that wider vision of worship with the local church. It involves having the courage and imagination to listen to the experiences of others in worship, and to learn from them; to be prepared to sit light to dearly held traditions (old and new) and to let other people grow in their worship. A parish worship group can help as much with the continued liturgical formation of those who conduct worship as of those who worship in the pew. Liturgical formation neither begins nor ends with formal theological training.

HISTORY

Such training in liturgy as existed for clergy prior to the foundation of the theological colleges in the late nineteenth century relied heavily upon oral tradition, the clergyman's ability to use and interpret the rubrics of the Book of Common Prayer, and the care (or lack of it) given to a new curate by his incumbent. It was something of a hit or miss affair, as contemporary accounts of inaudible services, indifferent sermons and general liturgical malaise bear witness. The influence of the Ritualist movement, and the foundation of the theological colleges, largely on party lines, served to heighten clerical and lay awareness of the importance of the practice of public worship, and of the clergy's role in its ordering. Legal wranglings over the minutiae of ritual were probably rather less important in the forming of late nineteenth- and early twentieth-century clergy than the party lines which were firmly taught and practised in churches and colleges of radically differing churchmanship and reinforced by the publication of annotated books on Anglican liturgical worship. All used the Book of Common Prayer, but Evangelicals remained vested in cassock, surplice, scarf and hood on all occasions, stood at the North End of the Holy Table, eschewed the use of candles or wafers at the Holy Communion, and advocated the primacy of the word, preached at Matins and Evensong as the principal Sunday services. Anglo-Catholics centred their worship on the Mass, as it became known, vested in alb, stole and chasuble, facing East, with full ceremonial, candles and wafers, and stressed the importance of the regular (weekly or daily) reception of the sacrament of the Holy Communion. Common prayer, such as it was, was simply to be found in the common texts of the Book of Common Prayer, where they were used. The styles of liturgical celebration varied very widely indeed. Arguments over the use of ceremonial and the interpretation of Prayer Book rubrics served to illustrate the importance of liturgical formation for the spiritualities of individuals and for the Church's self-understanding and identity.

CURRENT EXPERIENCE

The period of rapid liturgical revision, roughly 1960 to the present day, has coincided with a period of rapid social change and a revolution in the styles and content of theological training. Many ordinands in training today are aged between 30 and 45 years, are married, and often have children. A significant number have been in employment for at least ten years prior to the commencement of theological training. As a result, the student profile in residential colleges is quite mixed. Some colleges train men and women predominantly in their 20s and early 30s, on courses lasting on average three years. Other colleges, and all the non-residential courses, are characterised by a student profile of men and women over 30 years of age, on courses lasting an average of two to three years. Today the formative influences on ordinands are very likely to be found in the churches which they attended before beginning their college or course training; and in patterns of prayer geared around the demands of family life. Relatively few ordinands experience anything like the semi-monastic community life revolving around the corporate recitation of the offices and the eucharist which was the norm in colleges until the late 1960s. Instead, most ordinands in college training participate in a pattern of term-time daily prayer (usually based on ASB or BCP forms), often, but not exclusively, held corporately in the college chapel. This is supplemented by experience in parish and other pastoral placements. Some colleges provide a term-time framework of corporate liturgical worship which is obligatory for all students; others offer a pattern into which students opt by negotiation with their tutors. Ordinands training non-residentially on courses experience a mixture of their parochial (largely Sunday) pattern of liturgical worship, and the gatherings for worship provided at their residential weekends and annual summer schools, as well as placement experiences. Almost all ordinands in colleges and courses can expect to experience a greater or lesser degree of ecumenical forms of liturgical worship during the course of their training. Readers and other lay people who exercise responsibility for the conduct of public liturgical worship are not generally given any extra regular experience of liturgical worship as part of their training over and above what they normally experience week by week in their own churches.

One further factor which helps to shape the complexity of questions to do with liturgical formation in the 1990s is the age of those training for or already exercising active responsibilities for the conduct of public worship. For those ordained or licensed in or before the early 1960s (i.e. now in their early 50s or older) the Book of Common Prayer was the liturgical book of the Church of England. It may have been used in widely differing ways, and it may have been supplemented or used in revised forms; but the Book of Common Prayer texts were and are the primary formative liturgical texts for a generation of clergy and Readers who are still involved in active ministry today.

Clergy, Readers and others in their late 30s or 40s can still be expected to be more or less familiar with the Book of Common Prayer from their own early experiences of worship. But many who have been converted since the mid-60s, or who are now in their 20s or early 30s, will point to Series 2 or Series 3 or to the Alternative Service Book as their prime, or sole, formative liturgical text prior to their selection and training for ordination or licensing. For these men and women, the traditions inherent in the words and styles of conducting Book of Common Prayer liturgical worship may have to be learnt from scratch during formal theological training. For some others, often from largely quasi-liturgical Anglican churches, the notion of liturgical worship at all (let alone ASB or BCP forms) will be new to them as they begin training. The laments at the lack of 'common prayer' made in synods or the church press are often made in ignorance of the reality of the liturgical backgrounds from which significant numbers of today's ordinands and Readers are drawn.

The largely unanalysed and unrecorded influence of the experience of forms of liturgical worship by potential ordinands, Readers and others is one of the keys to their liturgical formation or lack of it. Yet this is not usually once-for-all but a continuing process of formation through experience; witness the effect attendance at Spring Harvest or Taizé can have on the theological and liturgical priorities of those who pattern and conduct public worship in the parish. Significantly, these experiences of worship are not confined to or even centred on formal periods of training, but often take place during the years prior to formal theological training, or can happen well after ordination or licensing. Clearly, there are also those where the influence of a particular form or style of worship is so formative that further change in attitudes or practice appears to be well-nigh impossible. In general, it is important not to underestimate the significance of this liturgical experience as formative of attitudes towards worship, and its public practice.

FORMAL TRAINING: COLLEGE, COURSE AND AFTER ...

The abolition of the General Ministerial Examination, and with this of centrally formed ordination syllabi, has created a significant new situation in the liturgical formation of ordinands. Considerable freedom has been given to the colleges and courses to develop the structures and content of the forms of liturgical education and training which they offer to students, subject to approval by the Advisory Board of

Ministry. No longer need questions of liturgical formation be seen solely in terms of formal lectures on liturgical history, or simply as a matter of inculcating the habit of reciting the daily offices, important though both those experiences remain for any ordinand today. Liturgical educators on courses and in colleges today may work closely with colleagues to develop experiential forms of learning in liturgical spirituality, in church history and worship, in pastoral liturgy. Clearly, with these freedoms goes the responsibility of the liturgical educators and their educational institutions to be well acquainted with liturgical developments in parishes.

At the same time the abolition of a centrally approved syllabus has its dangers. These may be compounded when training institutions cannot find staff with an adequate background in liturgical study and where course moderators do not have much familiarity with contemporary liturgical scholarship. It is important for the educators to have a good grounding in liturgical study as well as in the varieties of parochial worship. Student placements ought to be geared, at least in part, to the liturgical learning needs of the student. This may involve closer co-operation between college/course and local supervision of the liturgical aspects of parochial placements than has always been the case in the past.

If the experience of liturgical worship is key to liturgical formation, and if that experience has normally taken place over a number of years before a candidate for ordained or licensed lay ministry begins their training, one of the prime aims of any formal training in liturgy is to enable the student to reflect critically upon their experience in order to gain a theologically informed understanding of their own tradition(s). This can be done in the lecture room, but is probably better done through peer group discussion or written assessment. Guidance needs to be given about the type and scope of questions to be addressed, but the aim is to enable students to distance themselves from their experience and to evaluate it, so that when they share in that worship again they do so with a greater depth of understanding, and an appreciation of the tradition(s) which has formed them.

Those with responsibilities for the conduct of liturgical worship also need to be familiar with the varieties of forms of liturgical worship used in the Church of England and in other major Christian denominations. A sound grasp of the historical development of liturgical forms of worship gives a grounding in this area, as does the use of varieties of forms of liturgical worship during a student's training. Assessment can be geared to ensure that students have to familiarise themselves with basic Anglican texts, and with one or more other liturgical traditions. It is important that students should always be encouraged to discover why texts, architecture, musical forms etc, developed in the way they did historically and theologically, in order to understand something of the inheritance within which the Church worships and works today.

It is also important that students become familiar with agreed boundaries to liturgical worship, and the need to authorise forms of liturgical worship. In an overwhelmingly individualistic society, notions of corporate responsibility, and the catholicity of the Church as expressed to some degree in forms of worship, tend to be weak. Encouraging students to reflect on the links between questions of ecclesiology and liturgy, and the means by which those links are put into practice (canon law, rubrics, synodical authorisation etc.) can help to foster a greater sense of vision as to the place of the worship of the local church within the traditions of the wider Church.

Acquaintance with the basic resources for Anglican worship can come through historical and theological studies, but should never be left to chance. A working knowledge of the background of students is necessary in order to ensure that each one is enabled to handle, study and use books and other resources with which they may have previously been unfamiliar. At a minimum, students should know their way around the daily offices, initiation rites, eucharistic rites and the ordinals of the Book of Common Prayer (1662) and the Alternative Service Book, and its supplements. Clearly, the familiarity born of regular and long-term use may not come during a student's formal training, but only later as their ministry develops in one or more parishes.

This requirement of familiarity and confidence also relates to what might loosely be called 'presiding skills'. Once again, the needs of individual students vary widely in this area. Colleges and courses normally try to ensure that students are given some training in voice production and singing; and most will be involved in planning and conducting at least some acts of liturgical worship during their training. Preaching is taught in a variety of ways, mostly involving live preaching to a congregation, followed by detailed analysis and reflection with a tutor and fellow students. Presiding skills are fundamental to the good conduct of liturgical worship, but are difficult to learn during a short course of formal training. This is an area where the influence of the incumbent of a parish is paramount, for good or ill. There is a good case for those responsible for Continuing Ministerial Training and for Post-Ordination Training to lay on training days in 'Presiding Skills' for people who have been in the ministry one, five, or even twenty-plus years. In the case of those men and women who now act as training incumbents to curates, it is also particularly important that their training opportunities include attention being given to the learning of training skills, and not simply concentrating on what aspects of liturgical worship should be taught when. An incumbent might have any amount of good imaginative liturgical sense, but if it cannot be communicated effectively it is of little help to the curate. Such training days, and formal theological training, could be well supplemented by the production of imaginative and clear printed guidelines on 'how to conduct' different forms of worship.

Finally, what is perhaps the most important element of liturgical formation for many students during their training is learning how to pray the liturgy, often in ways which are quite new to them. In order to enable others to pray the liturgy, ordinands and others in training need themselves to develop their own liturgical spirituality. It may simply be a matter of a student learning the value and habit of praying the daily offices, and following the daily lectionary. It may be a more profound sense of how to listen to the 'music' of an act of worship and to interpret that sense of awareness in spontaneous prayer with and for the congregation. It may be a matter of recognising how gesture, posture and move-ment may create or break the attention of her own and a congregation's thanksgiving. Again, the development of a liturgical spirituality is and cannot be confined to formal training, but it may be highlighted there and require further thought and attention well after ordination or licensing.

CONCLUSIONS

Elsewhere in this collection of essays, an 'evolving core' of Anglican common prayer is analysed and discussed. Clearly, if 'common prayer' is not simply to do with the text of the Book of Common Prayer, those who conduct liturgical worship in the Church of England need to have an under-standing of what the evolving core is and its significance for the Church. The individual worshipper, leader of worship or liturgical student may only be dimly aware of an evolving core within their own experience. For example, a wor-shipper might wonder at the use of the BCP Magnificat and the Series 2 version of the Lord's Prayer during what is basically ASB Evening Prayer. Here is an example of an evolving core which contains certain key texts (old and new) within a recognisably Anglican liturgical pattern and ethos. Each worshipper will be familiar with their own church's particular 'core' material and pattern of worship. Yet the person conducting that worship needs to be familiar with the evolving core common to the wider Church, beyond the bounds of local traditions and customs. Opportunities to identify and to use such materials and patterns (as well as to read about them) need further development within courses, colleges and in-service training days. In this way the wider evolving core should be seen as a living well of the old and new from which the local church can draw and to which it can add.

Whilst theological colleges and courses clearly have an important part to play in familiarising students with the theory and experience of such a notion of evolving common prayer, the responsibility for liturgical formation does not begin and end with formal training for ministry. Diocesan Liturgical Committees, and those responsible for Post-Ordination Training and Continuing Ministerial Education in each diocese, can and ought actively to foster continuing liturgical formation in clergy, Readers and others who conduct public worship. As long ago as 1986, the House of Bishops strongly recommended that Diocesan Liturgical Committees should encourage a deeper understanding of the liturgy and should provide opportunities for clergy and laity alike to learn and assimilate the riches of Anglican liturgical spirituality.[1] Training days and refresher courses on presiding skills, the use of new liturgical material, structure and rhythm in worship, music, the use of space and movement in worship and so forth, are not simply interesting additions to a Post-Ordination Training or Continuing Ministerial Education programme – they are essential regular components of continued ministerial in-service training. Diocesan Liturgical Committees need to take their educational and consultancy roles seriously in the diocese, initiating diocesan, deanery and parish training days, in conjunction with diocesan training advisers and relevant para-church organisations, such as the Royal School of Church Music. If the Church's worship lies at the heart of the Church's mission, questions of continued liturgical formation cannot be left to chance. Properly constituted Diocesan Liturgical Committees can play a key part in fostering an evolving core of common prayer.

Diocesan Liturgical Committees also ought to function as the diocesan body advertising and promoting provincial or national liturgical training events or resources. Praxis now organises educational and training events not only in London, but in various venues around the country. Para-church organisations, such as the Church Pastoral Aid Society and the Church Union, organise occasional training days often in conjunction with the publication of major new liturgical resources. There is a good case to be made for Diocesan Liturgical Committees not simply being reactive to such events, but proactive: several Diocesan Liturgical Committees could work together with, for example, Praxis in promoting a planned series of events or consultancy opportunities for parishes or deaneries over a period of time.

In a different but related sphere, there is also a crying need for properly constituted opportunities to train and form liturgical scholars and teachers; those men and women who might teach in the theological faculties of universities, theological colleges and courses, and be available for advisory or educational work in dioceses and deaneries. At present, there is no university post in liturgical studies in the United Kingdom. Supervision of post-graduate liturgical studies is arranged by a few university theology faculties through no more than a handful of qualified liturgical scholars, who earn their living through other means. With its fine traditions, and the riches it has to offer not only the Anglican Church but ecumenical relations as well, Anglican liturgical scholarship needs concrete and well-founded funding. The establishment of a University post in liturgical studies, perhaps funded ecumenically, would bear much fruit in the future worshipping life of the Church.

Clearly there are many levels at which liturgical formation is needed by different ministers, from basic practical skills in the conduct of worship to the demands laid on ministers by the publication of innovative liturgical material such as that in the draft provisions published as *Patterns for Worship* (1989). It is no longer the case that a simple set order of service is published centrally, and the job of the minister is simply to read or sing the service. A good working knowledge of the pastoral and spiritual priorities within the congregation, a sense of the rhythms and patterns of worship in which the people have been formed, an understanding of the architectural and musical resources for the worship, a familiarity with the wealth of personnel and textual resources available – all these factors will need to be weighed by those who plan worship and who are sensitive to the needs and opportunities posed by the development of an evolving core of liturgical common prayer in the Church today.

JANE SINCLAIR

NOTES

[1] Liturgical Commission, 'The Need for Liturgical Committees' (Unpublished paper, 1986), p. 1. Copies of this paper can be obtained by Diocesan Liturgical Committees by writing to: The Secretary of the Liturgical Commission, Church House, Great Smith Street, London SW1P 3NZ.

11

Stability and Change:
Handling Liturgy in the Parish

LONGING FOR THE STABILITY OF THE PAST

We are witnessing an historic process that will inevitably change man's psyche. For across the board, our images of reality, responding to the acceleration of change outside ourselves, are becoming shorter-lived, more temporary. We are creating and using up ideas and images at a faster and faster pace. Knowledge, like people, places, things and organisations, is becoming disposable.[1]

Toffler's 1971 statement may be shown to be even more true twenty years later. But it is also true that there is a powerful backlash against change, or against some sorts of change. It is politically interesting that it is precisely those radical conservatives whose monetarist policies have contributed to the rapid rise and fall of industries and organisations, to a state of continual economic change, and to a shift in values in almost every sector of society away from the long-term good of society and individuals towards a short-term cash evaluation, who are adamantly against change in areas such as personal morality or religion. In the midst of the sea of change, there is a longing for some rocks and anchors which can hold us to the stability of the past. Is the worship of the Church necessarily cast in this role?

Toffler suggests three ways of coping with change which have interesting ecclesiological and liturgical implications.

First, there should be situational groupings of people passing through similar changes, e.g. groups for those moving house, getting married, and so on. The churches are already doing this, with groups for those preparing for marriage, for the baptism of their children, for the unemployed, the bereaved – and some of these have liturgical outcomes.

Second, he suggests the need for 'halfway houses' for those undergoing change, citing as examples those moving back into society from prison or mental hospital. The Church is already in the business of gradualising change, from helping to staff pre-retirement courses to using house groups, house communions, and family services as halfway houses into the Church. Here those undergoing the change from a non-Christian state to full-time following of Christ can make their adjustment to the new environment. And it is not insignificant that many joining a Christian group and making this kind of change do so at the point when other things in life are changing too, as they go to college, or move house, or have a baby, or lose a partner. In its strategic evangelism the Church is actually also meeting a societal need: would it be better equipped to do so if there were more specific (and therefore new!) liturgical provision which could be offered at such changes in life's stages?

Toffler's third suggestion is that there should be deliberate 'enclaves of the past', museum-piece societies where the rate of change is artificially depressed, where those suffering from shock-change can go and recuperate. Some both inside and outside the Church see us playing this role. And there is a very real sense in which coming to worship week by week should be an opportunity for healing from the hurts of our over-pressurized society, for stepping back and reassessing life through a different set of values, for escaping into the cocoon of a loving and stable set of relationships. This should have the effect of enabling people to find in God the strength they need to go out and fight for him, being his ministers in society for the next six days. It is dangerous when it does not seem to have this recuperating and re-equipping effect. Now the Church can do this without taking people back into the past, and does it best when it refuses to allow people to be simply nostalgic. The command, 'Do this in remembrance of me' is not nostalgic but a command to depend for our lives *now* on the death, resurrection and eternal presence of Jesus Christ. If the Church becomes a refuge, opting out of the fermenting change in society, the therapy it offers becomes irrelevant, and its ministry in society is reduced to a ministry to those who can't stand the pace. A glance at some of our congregations might reveal that this has already happened in some places. If it is simply an enclave of the past, there is no application of the living power of the risen Christ to the mass of men and women rushing headlong onwards in an ever-changing world, no living celebration in its worship of the delightfully varied and continuing creativity of God.

Whether or not the Church is involved in ministering in a changing society by helping to establish situational groupings, or by a deliberate policy of creating halfway houses, or by some controlled use of the 'enclaves of the past' idea, is not just a national question to be decided by synods and commissions, but one for every local church and clergyman. Either clinging to the past or cutting loose and going with the turbulent sea are easier, more understandable options to follow than some middle way which it has been our Anglican tradition to find. Few clergy are trained in the management of change, and many either cut adrift and get washed up and down aimlessly, or cling so tight to the anchor that the boat gets swamped and sinks. One of the problems of the recurrent BCP versus ASB debate is that people on both sides often assume that the Church is moving from one stable four hundred year old rite to another built to last the same length of time. But the real and usually unspoken hurt is that here, as in so many other areas in life, we are moving from a 'no change' situation to an 'all change' situation, where stability is not going to be achieved even after twenty years 'experiment'.

UNDERSTANDING THE BARRIERS TO CHANGE

The first step to managing change in the local church, whether in worship or anything else, is to understand and face the hurts and pains that change causes, and the barriers that result. There may be a local history of change being badly managed, the results of which may need uncovering and examining with groups of people in the church. It is the church together, rather than just the incumbent, which needs to learn the lessons from such a history.

There are a number of possible barriers that are worth exploring. *First, the loss of familiar spiritual language.* Most people make their own the language, ritual and music of the group in which they have their initial Christian experience, the group with which they identify, whether that be the family group from birth or the group in which they become Christians later. To lose this language, ritual and music is not only threatening: it can seriously damage people's spiritual health. Those who speak of their initial Christian experience in terms of the AV, and for whom the language of the BCP, much of it known by heart, has been the vehicle that carried them into God's presence both in public and in private devotion, suffer a severe spiritual jolt on moving to a church where there is none of this. No wonder people ask, 'where has my sense of God gone?', as both his identity and their identity are clouded by the absence of the familiar language.

This sense of loss seemed even more threatening to the continuance of spiritual life in the massive change from the Latin Mass experienced by the Roman Catholic Church. A significant letter to *The Tablet* in 1975 by the late David Jones outlined some now familiar problems: the suspicion of doctrinal change, the removal of the numinous, consequent changes and impoverishment musically, problems over dress '... the prevailing determination to be rid of the hieratic language of the Western rite, to change the rubrics which stressed the sacral character of what is either a profound and unfathomable mystery or nothing; to transfer the emphasis from propitiatory sacrifice to "commemorative meal", to somehow diminish whatever most evoked the numinous, to abandon the modal chant – that most superb of art-forms that the West has given to the world and which, incidentally, leads us back to the modal chant used in the Cenacle ... as also the laticlaved tunica of the deacon, the planeta of the celebrant, lead us visually back to that world of Antiquity.' And all these problems stem, according to David Jones, from the refusal of those introducing new liturgy to recognize that with no artefacture there is no Christian cult. Man is a sign-making animal and the sign-making, ritual, dress, and other art-forms of the Christian liturgy are its language. To sweep all that language away, with all its memory associations reaching far back into spiritual history, is very dangerous; more so in a technological society which sets little store by memory and has an impoverished sign-language. If we look in contemporary society for our signs (as did our early forefathers), they are few and continually changing because of the short-term memory of technological man.

Second, the arrival of the new vicar, seen as an 'incomer' in rural terms, complete with suburban presuppositions about the nature of the Church and a ready-made set of ideas and experiences which are at variance with those in the village church. The coming together of an era of liturgical change with a high degree of mobility and technology enables an even greater fluidity in liturgy. The new vicar arrives, and is freer than he ever has been to impose his own language, in words, ritual, church furnishings. It might come from his college, his last parish, the latest fashion, or a considered set of theological principles. It will be seen as a threat to the already existing language of the people. But he is able to do what he wants because there is no *one* already existing language (because of mobility), and because in a situation where the liturgical technologists have all but destroyed the traditional sign-language, his language is as good and has as long a history as anyone else's.

Stories about vicars abound, but two might illustrate the ham-fisted and the manipulating types.

The new vicar wandered around with a melancholy expression and had a very abrupt manner. At once he made it clear that he hadn't the remotest interest in church music. Mattins was abolished, and because the settings possessed by the church didn't fit the words of the new rite, sung eucharist went overboard. Never at any time did the vicar smile or speak cheerfully to the choir members; if he spoke at all it was to produce a series of complaints. After some particularly ham-fisted action by the vicar some of the choir decided to leave and the local newspaper took up the incident.

The congregation told the vicar that they were disturbed by various changes. He asked them to be more specific and they offered numerous suggestions, such as the fact that they no longer had the Litany, that they never heard the Ten Commandments, and so on. Mr X listened attentively, and promised to accede to their requests. The next Sunday morning there was procession, followed by Mattins, Litany and Ante-Communion, a long and erudite sermon about the practices of the ancient Church, and one of the exhortations that follows the Prayer for the Church Militant. Everything was taken at a leisurely pace and the congregation tottered out one and three-quarters of an hour later. Mr X was immensely pleased with himself; he remarked gleefully that he was prepared to bet that there would be no further requests from the people. He was right.

Both the ham-fisted and the manipulative vicar have a negative effect on change, making those who are against change more determined and making the next proposed change by themselves or someone else more difficult. Something needs to be done to stop blundering vicars emptying the church.

Third, there is the fear of creating a ghetto church, where only the initiated few know how to use the new words and music, and the barriers are up against anyone else until they have had a particular initiatory experience. If you cannot get there every week, you will not be able to keep up with the rate of change, and by next Christmas you will no longer feel a member of the church. The problem about the debate over folk religion is that it is too often seen in either-or terms. Either the vicar acts as local priest of the folk cult, adding his benign presence to all local events, blessing the sea, the corn, the pub and everything else in the community; never offends anyone, preaches in such a way as always to uphold and never to challenge the views and values of the majority in the community – and the cutting edge of the gospel of orthodox apostolic Christianity is blunted. Or the church feels – and expresses – criticism of those who come only for baptisms, weddings, funerals and Christmas, who only want the outward symbols or trappings of religion, and not the living reality of the faith; and so the only links with the community are grudging ones, the church is seen as being out of touch and irrelevant and, no longer being a focus for the religion of the community or having a prophetic or 'salt' ministry to it, becomes a eucharistic sect with a gathered church ecclesiology which belongs more traditionally to Baptists and Brethren than to the Church of England. And so, when the music and the preaching appear to follow the ecclesiology, the locals say, 'If we wanted to be Methodists, we'd have joined their church'. And part of the hurt is feeling not only that they no longer belong or feel at home in the local church, but that the church has, in some way, been taken away from the village community.

CLARIFYING THE VISION

When any particular change is contemplated, it is worth asking some questions which might help to refine and clarify what is really wanted. What is the motive for this change? Is it in line with the overall long-term objectives of the church? Is it likely to lead to division or to 'unchurching' some people in the church? For instance, if the overall long-term objective is an increase in the numbers in church through effective evangelism, part of which might be providing worship which is more 'accessible' to those outside the church, there might be some change proposed which is potentially divisive, such as transforming the first part of the eucharist into something with more of a 'family service' style. That potential division would not in itself mean that the change was inappropriate, but facing that possibility might determine the way in which such a change was introduced. Acknowledging the danger of division might, for instance, make the church reluctant to accept a change which was pushed through the PCC with only a slender majority.

Asking questions about the proposed change should also clarify how large a change it is, how far a departure from the church's tradition, and who the people are who are most likely to be affected. Some changes are very large, and affect everyone: for example, a proposal to demolish the building and to worship in local schools and pubs instead. Nearly as big in most people's minds would be a proposal for the complete re-ordering of the interior of the building. Next in the order of scale might be a wholesale change in services or worship books, from, say, 1662 to ASB, or a major change in the leadership of worship. Clearly both of these are capable of infinite gradation, from varying one option within the service to moving from the ASB to a set of service cards or a home-produced booklet, or from involving a group of people in leading the intercessions to sharing the effective presidency of the rite between a group of people which includes women. And the enormity of such proposals will vary from one church to another. So the questions we ask about a proposed change will include something about how acclimatised this church is to change, as well as the scale of change anticipated. We should also ask where the authority comes from for making such a change. The size and importance of an issue may be gauged from the fact that, for some changes, the Worship and Doctrine Measure states that there must be agreement between incumbent and PCC; or for some building changes the Care of Churches Measure requires a legal process involving agreement between them, the Diocesan Advisory Committee and the Chancellor of the Diocese. But there will be other changes for which the authority will be that of the PCC, or the minister taking the service.

The enormous variety of situations make it difficult to legislate on a national basis for all but the most major changes, but it is worth considering whether it might be possible to lay down basic principles for the introduction of most changes in the parish. This could be done, for instance, by changes to the Canons, the provision of guidelines, and a clear indication in our services as to which matters needed the approval of the PCC. Putting this into a legal framework would, however, need to be seen as a statement that the whole Church felt that this was important, rather than as a piece of legislation which could be enforced in the courts. Seeing canon law in this more traditional Roman Catholic way might in fact make it more useful and less divisive. And it needs to be remembered that even such a gentle extension of canon law into this area would still leave untouched other areas which have a greater effect on what a service feels like – the style of leadership of the minister, words and music of hymns, songs, instrumental solos, the way the sermon is preached (by one or more people, with audio visuals, interviews or group discussion)...

This process of asking questions should result not only in clarifying the vision of what is to be changed, but also in clarifying who needs to be consulted and whose approval it is advisable to have: in other words, it will begin to determine the process to be used in bringing the change about. But before we move to discuss the process, there is another dimension to explore in clarifying the vision, namely looking at theology, or the Bible, or our wider Christian tradition, or asking God what he might think of it.

Because of the natural human tendency to stray away from God-given principles, the Church needs continually to look again at what was originally handed down, and to allow its current practice to be judged by that light. This means that any change will be judged, not by what is fashionable or by what the rest of the world does, but by scripture and by the practice of the early Church. Examples of this abound – the recovery of the doctrine of the Church as the body of Christ, evidenced in the Peace, the eschatological emphases in the ASB eucharist when compared with 1662, the enrichment of the Thanksgiving, changes in furnishings and in services which show the family nature of Christian worship. The Church of England as it now is sometimes needs to be reminded of its reformation principle of *ecclesia semper reformanda*: but that does not mean that the Church should be in a continual state of turmoil to keep abreast with current society. The Church also needs to take a fresh grasp of that other reformation principle, *sola scriptura*. In other words, change and the movement towards it need to be principled and not unprincipled or solely for the sake of fashion. So what kind of theological principles might we look at?

We could do worse than start with the nature of God. We serve a God who is a God of change, continually doing new things. 'He controls the times and the seasons; he makes and unmakes kings' (Dan. 2. 21). 'Now I will tell you of new things even before they begin to happen. Sing a new song to the Lord.' (Isa. 42. 9, 10). 'This cup is the new covenant in my blood ...' (1 Cor. 11. 25). And he not only changes the world, but demands change in the hearts, minds and lives of those he has created.

But God is also one who never changes. He says through the prophet Malachi, 'I am the Lord and I do not change' (Mal. 3. 6). The psalmist says about the heavens and earth which God created, 'They will disappear, but you will remain; they will all wear out like clothes . . . But you are always the same, and your life never ends' (Ps. 107. 26). The unchanging nature of God is in no way protected, reflected or guaranteed by unchanging worship or unchang-

ing people any more than it is by an unchanging country-
side. What people need as a rock and anchor in the midst of
change is a relationship with the only one who does not
change: that is their only ultimate security.

In this context, further theological reflection on the
nature of God should lead to some worship-oriented questions. Why does he want us to worship? Does he need our
worship? What kind of worship? The prophets talk about
him having no use for bulls and goats, but does that mean
the use of the concept of sacrifice is a non-starter? And does
this talk about justice and having clean hands, or about
making peace with your brother on the way to worship,
have anything to say to us about God being interested in the
everyday world of our society at precisely the most holy
high point of our worship? And how, in all that, do you
recognise where he is? How do you know he is listening?
Or answers prayer? Is there some way of 'capturing' his
presence and knowing he is here, or do we just work very
hard at creating some sense of the numinous with the
materials at our disposal – beautiful words, distant views, art
and music, colour, smell and silence? And in the light of this
kind of reflection, what difference could any change that we
might devise possibly make?

Two further areas suggest themselves for theological
reflection: the doctrine of the Church, and the doctrine of
the ministry. Each of these will affect both the vision for
change itself, and also the process by which that change is
achieved. People work with different models of the
Church, and with different models of the ministry. It would
seem only right to be open about this, and, if we are
seeking principled change rather than change for whim and
fashion, to examine whether the proposed change is consistent with the model of Church or ministry currently held
by this particular church[2] and, if not, whether that is
deliberate or not. So, for example, it would be entirely consistent for a church working on the basis of a family model,
with the aim of reaching out to families and involving them

in the worshipping life of the church, to make changes to make its worship more inter-generational, for instance to propose to involve families in leading intercessions together. But it would not be as consistent for such a proposal to come from a church working with a 'herald' model, where the clarity of what was proclaimed in the service might well be impeded by some mumbling from the youngest child, forgiven and part of the 'message' in the family-model church, but criticised as unprofessional and unclear in the herald-model church.

But as well as asking whether the vision for change is consistent with the basic model of Church and ministry, an examination of these should also help determine the process by which change is achieved. Having a high doctrine of the Church as the people of God together, or as the interdependent and whole body of Christ, should inhibit individual leaders from taking the initiative in imposing change: rather, it should point towards some kind of process which carries the whole body of the church together. And the minister is there in the community as the prophet sharing the vision, the educator teaching about the need for the vision, and the enabler of the process which brings it about – and in a church with the 'body' model the minister will be sharing the exercise of those ministries with others.

Both Catholics and Evangelicals can behave as if they were autocratic popes exercising absolute sway over their people – who would often have it so. But each needs to be asked some questions about the theology of ministry: about the servant nature of the priesthood and ministry of Christ, and the position of the minister as part of the *laos* of God.

And it is in the interaction of these two bits of theology, about the Church and about the ministry, that questions of trust and authority arise. Where does authority lie for this particular change? With the congregation or with its leader? Those with management skills use a simple chart ranging from leader-dominant to group-dominant. The point at which this particular action is taken will be determined not only by the views of the leader and the group, but by the nature and urgency of the action. If the proposal is very long-term, with plenty of time for teaching, consultation and changing of views, then the leader can be in highly collaborative mode. But if the situation is urgent, and the leader possesses knowledge and the authority to take action – if, for example, there is a fire in the building – then he will be absolutely authoritarian in spelling out what should happen. Sometimes the church is in such a desperate situation, facing virtual destruction, that an authoritarian approach may need to be used, with a view to bringing about a changed situation in which a more collaborative style can be used.

DETERMINING THE PROCESS

The process of handling change in the liturgy in the parish will involve for the leadership of the local church a time of understanding the barriers and hurts which change involves, and of clarifying the vision for change. The leadership will then need to determine a process which will acknowledge the barriers and hurts, and perhaps deal with some of them, and which will enable the vision to be clarified and decisions to be taken, implemented and evaluated.

Some of the fears about change have specific answers. The fear about losing familiar spiritual language can be at least partly helped by looking at ways of valuing and including ancient language 'enclaves of the past', not only in retaining some 'refuge' services which do not change while the church goes through a period of change, but by including such enclaves within both formal worship and informal occasions – mixing ancient hymns, anthems and prayers in a modern service, or retaining ancient actions and music sometimes when the words have changed. Such a mixture of ancient and modern within one structure is specifically provided for in the *Patterns for Worship*[3] structure.

Another area to explore is the use of the new language in the same way as the old, by encouraging people to learn parts of the service by heart and to use them in private and family devotions.

The fears about the manipulative and ham-fisted vicar, and the fear of creating a ghetto church, should be dealt with if the theological process described above is followed. But neither the ham-fisted nor those with a ghetto mentality are likely to follow such a process, and so other ways have to be explored. There are clear legal safeguards, embodied in the Worship and Doctrine Measure and in the Canons,[4] which are there to prevent a congregation from being bulldozed into unwanted change, and to enable the parties to a wedding, for instance, to choose the rite they feel is most suited to them. Do we need more publicity about these, or a code of practice or change in the canons to ensure that there is consultation and agreement not only about the rite used, but also about substantial changes to the contents by selecting different options? But, in addition to the law, there is the continuing pressure of peer groups in chapters, continuing ministerial education, and the effect both of young curates with a different approach to church life and of bishops and archdeacons with a vision of the wider good of the Church.

As well as the particular, there are other general factors involved in planning a process for change: timing and speed; the need for teaching and reflection and for a broad basis that ensures that the whole church is heading in the same direction. Who is to see the vision, set the goals, order the priorities? Who takes the initiative? If we hold to the unity of the church, we shall want the whole church to be involved in this exercise. Even if, in the present situation, it is likely that the vicar or leadership group will take the initiative, they should be open to God using other people as well. As a congregation becomes more liturgically and biblically aware, initiatives may arise which are seen to be absolutely right even though they were not part of the original vision. This will be more possible if the church is not seen to be following the programme of a particular vicar, but responding to the leading of God, in sharing in a day of prayer or in a day conference to consider the different options open to the church. If it is the vicar or leadership group who have the vision, they should share as much as they can. It does not help to have a 'hidden' programme or agenda, even though people sometimes withhold from the congregation where they are ultimately going, on the grounds that some of the congregation cannot cope with such a big picture of change. In fact they may be more likely to accept some changes if they can see them as part of a whole plan, consistent with a model of the church which is the basis for all other church activities as well.

Time is needed for people to share, catch and understand a vision, at each stage of this process. Some of the greatest hurts and worst mistakes in introducing change happen because those initiating it are in too great a hurry. Time is needed for assimilating and understanding what is proposed, which in many cases will be done by spending time talking to other people and to God about it. It may well be best, for instance, if the PCC hears the presentation and has some initial discussion, but then defers further discussion and decision to the next meeting. The PCC may then proceed in a number of different ways, of which the following are some:

Delegating responsibility to a worship committee or an ad hoc group or the clergy may be the right course to take with some things that are not too enormous. Such a group might try different options in the service, or vary the visual appearance of the church in terms of the ministers' dress, frontals, banners and flower arrangements; or it might try various different things with the music, different instruments or different communion settings for instance. If responsibility is delegated in this way the PCC should probably set some time at which it will comment on what has been happening. This is essential if what is delegated is the job of experimenting with things so that the PCC, having seen the different options, can come to a decision. If there is to be experimentation, the time must be long enough for the experiment not simply to be regarded as a novelty, and for different variations to be tried. For instance, in experimenting with *Lent, Holy Week, Easter* it would not be sufficient just to do one of each of the services.

Setting up a working party or committee is the usual 'if in doubt' policy. At the exploratory stage of sharing and testing the vision this works best if it is a very small group, not necessarily all of the same persuasion, but with some chance of not debating everything for hours and hours. They will then be less likely to come back to the PCC with an agreed plan in which they all have a very high stake because of the hours of negotiation invested in it. At the next stage, when the PCC has made its decisions in principle and the job is one of representing things to the congregation and managing the introduction of the change, it might work better to have a larger committee, representative of the different groups within the church.

This initial working group should have the job (given in clear terms of reference by the PCC) of doing a sort of feasibility study. This may involve looking at what other churches do, seeking advice from outside the church, making lists of options and sounding out the congregation, assessing resources for making this particular change in terms of good will, manpower, money, time. The group may also be responsible for some or all of the following ways of taking the matter further.

Teaching about a change in sermons or in other groups may be essential to a particular change. Listening to what scripture has to say may convince some and inspire others to suggest further allied changes. And as well as teaching about a particular proposed change, some theological reflection about the nature of God, the Church and the ministry in relation to change, along the lines suggested earlier, should ensure that changes have a thorough basis.

Discussion in house groups may be one way of finding out what some ordinary church members feel – and that may be part of the decision-making machinery, with the house group leader reporting the overall feeling of his group about a suggested change. Discussion notes may be prepared, and members of the working group, or one person, may visit each house group.

Questionnaires may be compiled and either handed out to church members or used as the basis for interviews of the congregation conducted by the working group.

Leaflets and other publicity may be produced – not too permanent-looking if the PCC is not to give the impression that its mind is made up. Pictures and diagrams help. A time during the notices in church may be used, with visuals to help people understand the proposals, or an interview with someone who knows what the effect of a proposed change might be, for instance the organist in connection with a musical change. Parish magazine and local press may be used to bring to the attention of the local community any change which may be relevant to them.

Decision-making: The process of sharing the vision and gathering responses, perhaps changing the vision as the discussion proceeds, merges into the process of decision-making as a large number of people get involved in agreeing to share the vision or wanting to go for a different one. For major decisions there might be a call to a day of prayer, and to look for some specific indication that God is moving the whole church in one direction. Some churches would not move unless there was some indication of this, such as a unanimous vote on the PCC.

Communication, Implementation, Evaluation: Once the decision is taken, it needs to be communicated in as many ways as possible to the congregation and to any others affected. Some kind of management group – the PCC, the working group or the worship committee – might handle the introduction of the change, depending on its size, with a presentation to the congregation on the reasons and benefits to be derived from it. Possibly the same group should also be responsible for monitoring and evaluating the change.[5]

TREVOR LLOYD

NOTES

[1] Alvin Toffler, *Future Shock* (Bodley Head: London 1970).

[2] Churches, of course, operate with different models at different stages of their life, and some operate with different models at the same time as they engage with different situations: this may well emerge as there is some principled theological discussion of the basis for change.

[3] *Patterns for Worship:* A Report by the Liturgical Commission, GS 898 (Church House Publishing: London 1989), pp. 16-29.

[4] See *Public Worship in the Church of England*: A guide to the law governing worship and doctrine in the Church of England (General Synod: London 1986), pp. 3-5 & 7-8, and Canons B 3 and B 5.4.

[5] I have written in more detail on some of the topics covered in this essay in my *Introducing Liturgical Change,* Worship Series 87 (Grove Books: Bramcote, Notts, 1979).